Simple Weaving

Simple Weaving

Hilary Chetwynd

Studio Vista London
Watson-Guptill Publications New York

For Mary Keer

Cover Coat or dress fabric. Warp 11 cut orange tweed wool. Reed 8. 16 warp ends per inch. Weft 11 cut orange tweed wool and 1½'s orange looped mohair

Title page Section of wall hanging. Warp 2/6's (6/2's) dark green cotton. Reed 8. 16 warp ends per inch for 1". 2½" space. Weft 4/4's black dressed cotton and natural garden cane

General Editors Brenda Herbert and Janey O'Riordan
© Hilary Chetwynd 1969
Published in London by Studio Vista Limited
Blue Star House, Highgate Hill, London N19
and in New York by Watson-Guptill Publications
165 West 46th Street, New York 10036
Distributed in Canada by General Publishing Co. Ltd
30 Lesmill Road, Don Mills, Toronto, Ontario
Library of Congress Catalog Card Number 69–13174
Set in Univers 689 9 on 9½pt
by V. Siviter Smith and Co. Ltd, Birmingham
Printed in the Netherlands
by N.V.Grafische Industrie, Haarlem
SBN 289.37066.3

Contents

Bibliography

A Handweaver's Pattern Book by Marguerite Porter Davison.
Published by the author, Swarthmore, Pennsylvania, USA

The Weaver's Craft by L. E. Simpson and M. Weir.
Dryad Publications

Handbook of Textile Fibres by J. Gordon Cook, B.Sc., Ph.D.
Merrow Publishing Co. Ltd

Woven Cloth Construction by A. T. C. Robinson and R. Monks.
The Textile Institute

K. R. Drummond, supplier of weaving books and magazines.
30 Hart Grove, Ealing Common, London W.5

Museum Books, Inc., weaving books and magazines.
48 East 43rd Street, New York, N.Y. 10017

Handweaver and Craftsman, weaving magazine.
220 Fifth Avenue, New York, N.Y. 1001

New Key to Weaving by Mary E. Black. Bruce Publishing Co.,
Milwaukee, Wisconsin

The Technique of Woven Tapestry by Tadek Beutlich.
Watson-Guptill Publications, New York and
B. T. Batsford Ltd., London

Handloom Weaving by Luther Hooper. Pitman

The Textile Arts by Verla Birrell. Harper and Brothers, New York

Introduction

Weaving can be a really creative and imaginative craft, as well as a practical one. Many weavers seem to worry so much about the technicalities of the craft that they forget the creative opportunities they have at their finger tips.

An industrial designer of woven textiles creates ideas to be mass-produced by machine. A hand weaver does not have this limitation, and is able to produce exciting fabrics which cannot be woven by machine, or are not usually woven by machine.

The hand weaver is restricted only by the limitations of his own hand loom, and with some experimentation it is surprising what a variety of ideas a hand loom can produce. This is of particular importance to a weaver hoping to sell his work. These days he cannot expect to compete with a machine, or to market a fabric similar to a mass-produced article at a higher price simply on the grounds that it is hand-woven. The weaver's customer is likely to be attracted to a fabric he is unable to buy on the open market, and is generally prepared to pay a fair price for an original creative idea.

Before the weaver or beginner launches onto weaving a long length, it is a good idea to weave a sample first and to explore the weave or technique thoroughly to see if he can make it more interesting with original design ideas of his own, rather than simply to follow instructions from a book.

The point at which a beginner should start weaving depends more on space, time, purpose and production than on the amount of experience he has previously had. It is not much more difficult to start weaving on a big foot-power (floor) loom than it is on a small table loom. The basic process is exactly the same, and adults sometimes find small looms too restricting for comfort.

A 24" wide, four-shaft (harness) table loom is a good size for weaving. A table loom any larger is usually too heavy to keep moving off the table, and takes up nearly as much space on the floor, whereas a foot-power (floor) loom takes up the same amount of space and is much easier and quicker to weave on. All foot-power (floor) looms are made to take to pieces, and can be stored more easily than a wide table loom.

A loom is a frightening object to anyone contemplating learning to weave, but setting up a loom in preparation for weaving is a methodical process always done the same way, and is not as slow and trying as it appears.

Drafting on graph paper is also an alarming-looking process, but this is not as difficult as it looks. All weavers and beginners should try it, as it is an important method of bridging the gap between the original design idea and the actual fabric. It is frus-

Fig. 1 Rigid heddle loom. Dryad Handicrafts

trating for the weaver if he is unable to try an idea because he does not know how to thread the loom for it. He can also try out designs on graph paper when no loom is available.

The weaver should have an open mind; he must always be prepared to try out weaves and have fun experimenting with unusual weaving materials and design ideas.

Weaving is an exciting hobby for a beginner because it is possible to make a variety of really useful articles on simple weaving equipment which can be made to fit on to a reasonable sized table. These articles can be made to be worn or to be used in the home. Once the first article has been woven, the weaver will have gained confidence and experienced a great sense of achievement. The excitement of the beginner when he comes to decide what to weave next can be intense. He will have already discovered that mixing colours with threads is quite unlike mixing colours in paint, and have become interested in the selection of coloured yarns. He will soon find himself increasing his weaving equipment to enable him to develop his sk'll over a wider area of handwoven textiles. The same honeycomb design has been used as an example throughout the book, which will enable the beginner to follow the instructions more easily.

Glossary

Beating in weft Forcing the last weft yarn placed in the warp shed up to the edge of the fabric with the reed or rigid heddle.

Countermarches or lamms Placed between the shafts and the pedals on a foot-power (floor) loom, for spacing the pedals and enabling the shafts to be raised and lowered evenly.

Heddle Heald. See p. 12.

Jack or rising-shed loom Foot-power loom used by handweavers in the U.S.A. This loom has the same action as a table loom, but the shafts are lifted by yokes attached to the pedals.

Leno twist Weave in which the warp threads are made to cross, sometimes known as gauze weave.

Plain weave Basic weave, in which the weft passes over and under alternate warp threads. Sometimes known by handweavers as tabby.

Raddle Used for spacing the threads before rolling the warp on to the back roller of the loom. See I p. 13.

Reed The warp threads are placed through a reed to determine the number of threads per inch. See J p. 14.

Roller shuttle Weft-yarn bobbin holder used to insert weft yarn, by allowing the yarn to trail behind as the shuttle passes through the shed of the separated warp threads.

Shaft Heald frame holding wire or cotton healds, through which the warp is threaded to take part in making a pattern in the fabric and to form a shed for weaving.

Shed Opening formed when the warp threads are separated by lifting or lowering the shafts when weaving.

Selvedge Double threads to give strength to the edges of a fabric, so that they will remain straight in weaving and finishing.

Treadling Action of pressing down a pedal on a foot-power loom to separate the warp threads to form a shed for weaving.

Tweed yarn A fairly coarse, rough yarn made from wool in a variety of weights and qualities; the fibres do not lie parallel.

Warp Threads of the same length parallel to one another in preparation for weaving. Threads lying along the length of a fabric after it is woven.

Weft Yarn intended for use in weaving. Threads across the width of a fabric after it is woven.

Worsted yarn A strong, lustrous, smooth yarn made from the long fibres of certain breeds of sheep. The fibres are spun from combed wool and lie parallel.

Looms

Fig. 2 Four-shaft (harness) 24"-wide table loom. Harris Looms

Rigid heddle loom

A simple loom which weaves only plain weave, with the warp always set in the heddle at 13 threads per inch. This loom is suitable for beginners and children aged eight years and upwards. Supplied in 9", 15" and 20" widths (Fig. 1 p. 8).

Two-way (harness) table loom

This two-shaft (harness) loom weaves only plain weave, but has an automatic action of the shafts (harnesses) which enables the weaver to work with more ease and speed than on a rigid heddle loom. Different reeds may be used, allowing the weaver to have any number of warp threads per inch. This loom is also suitable for beginners and children and is usually available in a 12" to 24" width.

Four-shaft (harness) table loom

A loom designed to weave plain and patterned fabric, using any number of warp threads per inch, with an automatic action of the shafts obtained by pressing levers at the side or centre of the loom. Supplied in 8", 15", 20", 24", 32" and 45" widths (Fig. 2).

Fig. 3 Four-shaft (harness) foot-power (floor) loom. Harris Looms

Four-shaft (harness) foot-power (floor) loom

Similar to a four-shaft table loom, but with the automatic action of the shafts (harnesses) controlled by pressing pedals with the feet. This enables the weaver to have his hands free for weaving and allows him to work with more ease and speed than on a table loom. Especially useful when weaving wide widths and long lengths of fabric (Fig. 3).

Refer to the chart (Fig. 4) for essential and non-essential weaving accessories for all looms. This may help a beginner to find out the initial cost of weaving. The accessories are described in Weaving Accessories p. 12.

Fig. 4 Accessories

Accessories	A	B	C	D	E	F	G	H	I	J	K	L	M	N	O	P	Q	R	S	T	U	V	W	X
Rigid heddle loom		●	●			●		0			●	●		●	0				●			●	●	●
Two-way loom		0	●	0	0		0	●	●	●		●		●		0			●	●		0		●
Table loom up to 24" wide			0	●	0	0		0	●	●	●		●		●		0	0	●	●	0			●
Table loom over 24" wide		0	0		0	0		0	●	●	●		●		●	●	0	0	●	●	0			●
Foot-power loom	●	0	0		0	0		0	●	●	●		●	0	●	●	0	●	●	0	●			●

● Essential   0 Non-essential

Weaving accessories

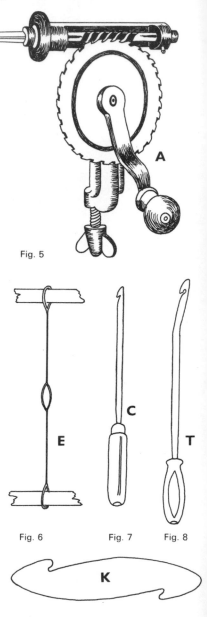

A Bobbin winder is essential for making bobbins of yarn to fit inside a roller (boat) shuttle when weaving lengths of fabric of 24" wide and over (Fig. 5).

B Drum for finishing woollen fabric. See page 101.

C Fine threading (reed) hook used for threading the warp threads through a rigid heddle. A useful hook, which can be used for threading any type of loom (Fig. 7).

D Flat wooden shuttle which has the weft yarn wound round it and is used for passing the weft yarn through the warp. One or two are provided with the loom, but it is usually necessary to have a few more.

E Heals (heddles) are made of heald (heddle) string, wire or metal, with an eye in the centre through which a warp thread is passed, so that its movement may be controlled when weaving. These are already threaded on the shaft (harness) frame of the loom, but it is a good idea to have some extra heals (heddles), since more may be required for weaving finer fabric (Fig. 6).

Fig. 5

Fig. 6   Fig. 7   Fig. 8

Fig. 9

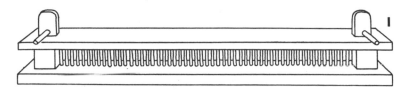

Fig. 10

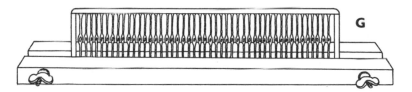

Fig. 11

Fig. 12

F Heald (heddle) string is useful in case it is necessary to make an extra heald (heddle) on shafts (harnesses) when a threading mistake has to be corrected (see Fig. 81 p. 48).

G Heddle holder is used placed across a rigid heddle loom to hold the heddle in an upright position for threading. It is also useful for holding the reed in the same position on a table when threading short lengths of yarn for designing the warp. The holder can be made easily with two lengths of wood about 2" × 1", with holes drilled through each end of both pieces for two wing nuts and bolts 3" long (Fig. 12).

H Loom cord is used in certain types of looms—thin cord for table looms and thick cord for foot-power (floor) looms. It is advisable to have loom cord in hand in case of breakages, as ordinary string does not last. In England Harris Looms have replaced loom cord with chain, which is obtainable from them or a hardware store. In the United States nylon cord, which is much stronger than loom cord, is generally used.

I Raddle is essential for spacing the warp threads to the correct width when placing the warp on the back roller of the loom. A raddle should be the same length or longer than the width of the loom. To make a raddle use a length of wood approximately 1" × $1\frac{1}{2}$", mark off half inches in pencil along the length, and hammer in $1\frac{1}{4}$" nails to a depth of about $\frac{1}{2}$", staggered to prevent the wood from splitting (Fig. 11).

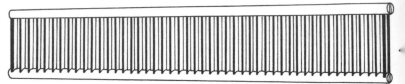

Fig. 13

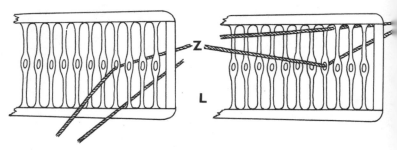

Fig. 14

J Reed consists of a number of wires closely set between two slats, and serves several purposes: separating the warp threads, guiding the shuttle, beating in the weft and, most important of all, determining the number of warp threads per inch. Reeds are bought to correspond with the width of the loom and with a number of dents desired per inch. A dent is the space between the wires, therefore an 8 reed has 8 spaces or dents per inch, a 10 reed has 10 dents per inch and so on. Since it is unnecessary to buy a whole range of different reeds to start weaving, begin with two reeds, an 8 and a 14, and continue buying as required. One reed will be supplied with the loom, usually an 8 or a 14 (Fig. 13).
K Reed hook is used for threading the warp threads through the reed (Fig. 9).
L Rigid heddle is used only on rigid heddle looms, and is always supplied with the loom. It acts as heals (heddles) and reed combined. Plain weave is obtained by raising the heddle and so lifting alternate warp threads (Z on Fig. 14) for weaving one weft thread, and then holding the heddle down which lowers the same warp threads (Z) for weaving the second weft thread (Fig. 14).
M Scissors, ordinary scissors.

N Shaft (harness) holder is useful for fixing the shafts (harnesses) in a level position when threading a foot-power (floor) loom and tying up the counter-marches (lamms) and pedals. Two can be made from lengths of wood $1\frac{1}{2}'' \times \frac{1}{2}''$ about 6" long (Fig. 17).

O Shed or cross (lease) sticks are placed through the cross of the warp to keep the threads in the correct order for threading and weaving. These are supplied with a shaft (harness) loom; but can be made, with two lengths of $\frac{3}{8}'' \times 1''$ wood cut to the length of the outside width of the loom, drilled with holes at each end and made smooth with sandpaper (Fig. 18).

P Shuttles are for passing the weft thread quickly through the warp when weaving, and only essential for weaving fabric 24" wide and over, especially on foot-power (floor) looms; otherwise flat wooden shuttles are satisfactory. 12" roller (boat) shuttles are the most adaptable, but note that these are useless without a bobbin winder (Fig. 5) for filling the shuttles (Fig. 16).

Q Skein winder or swift is useful for making a warp directly from a hank of yarn. The wooden one of Scandinavian design is

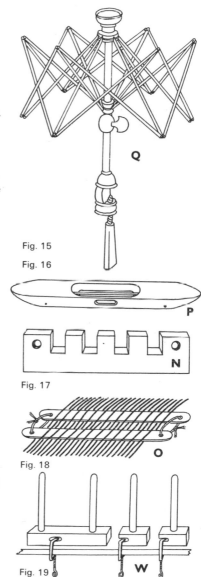

Fig. 15

Fig. 16

Fig. 17

Fig. 18

Fig. 19

15

decorative, but not a
necessity (Fig. 15).

R Spool rack is for holding
spools of yarn and allowing
them to rotate. This is useful,
but not essential for working
on looms of 24" width and
under, since the spool may
be placed in a box or jar.
A spool rack can be made
with a frame 30" × 18" of
$\frac{5}{8}$" × 5" wood, with holes
drilled down the centre of
the long sides to take $\frac{1}{4}$"
dowels of wood or metal on
which to slide the spools,
and two extra lengths of
wood 18" long screwed
across one of the short sides
of the frame to form a steady
base (Fig. 20).

S Stool of a correct and
comfortable height,
especially for foot-power
(floor) looms, can save
energy when weaving. An
ordinary kitchen stool is
often the answer. A simple
way to make a weaving
stool is with 1" × 12" wood,
two lengths of 22" and two
lengths of 18" (Fig. 21).

T Threading hook for
threading the warp threads
through the heald (heddle)
eyes. The correct way to use
this hook is with the hook
facing downwards (Fig. 8
p. 12).

U Warping board or frame is
for arranging threads up to
ten yards in length
parallel to one another, in

Fig. 20

Fig. 21

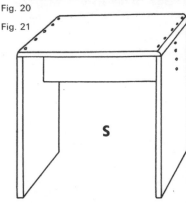

Fig. 22

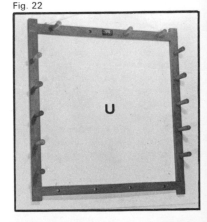

16

preparation for being placed on the loom. The board is a wooden frame with $\frac{1}{2}$" holes along the sides, in which to place pegs for making a warp to the required length. This can be made quite simply with wood approximately $1\frac{1}{2}" \times 2"$, and is used flat on a table or hanging on a wall (Fig. 22).

V Warping mill (reel or drum) has adjustable pegs for making warps anything up to 30 yards for a loom wider than 24" (Fig. 23).

Fig. 23

W Warping posts and clamps are fixed to the edge of a table for making a warp. They are suitable for anyone using a rigid heddle or two-way loom for making small articles (Fig. 19 p. 15).

X Warp sticks are slats of wood the same length as the back roller of the loom, used at intervals between the warp and the back roller when rolling the warp on the loom. This prevents the threads on the outside edges of the warp from falling off each other. More are usually needed than the few supplied with the loom. To make warp sticks buy wood approximately $\frac{1}{4}" \times 1"$ and saw into the required lengths. In place of warp sticks heavy wrapping paper or corrugated paper can be used, but this will not support the threads at the sides of the warp as successfully as warp sticks.

Yarns for weaving

Yarns for warp

The warp threads are placed on the loom and run down the length of the fabric, therefore the yarn must be reasonably strong.

The only threads unsuitable for the warp are single threads which have not been plyed, with the exception of tweed wool soaked in oil or certain fancy spun yarns. If a fancy spun yarn slips or breaks when rubbed firmly along the thread between thumb nail and finger, it should not be used for warp.

It is not advisable, especially for beginners, to make a warp with a mixture of fibres, such as wool and cotton, or cotton and linen, as (apart from silk and wool) the amount of elasticity varies in different yarns and makes the tension of the warp uneven.

Wool

Wool is one of the most useful and attractive yarns for weaving and especially suitable for beginners. Available in England, Cheviot tweed wool and Welsh tweed wool are single yarns, not plyed, soaked in oil to preserve the wool and to hold the fibres together for weaving. Do not be discouraged if the tweed fabric feels hard and the colour appears dull, this changes when it is washed and the oil removed. In the United States, use any 2/20's worsted, which is a good strong yarn for suiting and other fashion fabrics in a wide range of colours.

Other wool and worsted yarns have usually been plyed, and many of them have already been scoured. They are supplied in spools, cones and hanks. Ordinary knitting wools may be used for weaving, but, as they tend to look dull and flat, it is better to use a more interesting thread obtained from a supplier of yarns. 2-ply carpet yarn is useful for mixing with other wools, and as weft in cotton warps for furnishing fabrics.

Cotton

Cotton is slightly stronger than wool, but not as elastic or pliable. It is used mainly for table mats, curtains and other furnishing fabrics. Try using a cotton warp with a plyed wool or worsted weft for upholstery, cushion covers and table mats. This combination of yarn makes an attractive fabric which is very hard wearing and feels better than an all-cotton fabric.

Linen

As linen is a difficult yarn to handle, it is advisable for a beginner not to attempt using linen until he has had some experience with wool and cotton. Linen has little elasticity, and the threads tend to sag if there is any unevenness of tension in the warp. The warp has to be made and placed on the loom with care, and must be made of a plyed yarn, however strong the yarn may appear.

Silk

Silk is a beautiful yarn, surprisingly elastic, easy to handle, and rarely fails in a design due to its natural quality. The thread is rather fine, so it is better for a beginner to work with wool and cotton first, before handling quite as many threads in the warp as silk usually requires. Try using a mixture of wool and silk in the warp. Alternate threads of silk and wool will make a lovely fabric and will also make it possible to use silk, since it is expensive.

Man-made and chemical fibres

Do not be afraid to use man-made or chemical fibres after learning to weave with natural fibres. They are so strong that the warp threads will break the loom before the weaver will break the threads!

Yarns for weft

The weft threads run width-ways in a fabric with as many or fewer threads per inch than in the warp, therefore the threads may be thicker than the warp. Some weft threads are used mainly for decoration and need not be very strong. When this is the case, it is important to use a stronger yarn as well, or the warp yarn in combination with the decorative yarn in the weft, to make a good quality of fabric. Judgement of quality can be learnt from looking at and feeling the fabric. Creative ideas and decorations may be woven with a variety of materials not necessarily obtainable from a yarn supplier.

Designing the warp

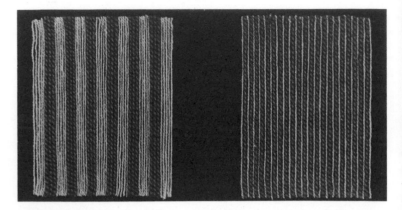

Figs. 24–25

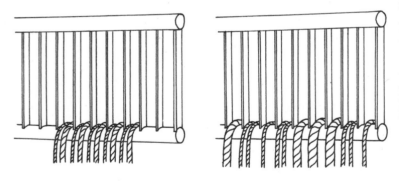

Fig. 26   Fig. 27

When selecting the yarns for the warp, a beginner is wise to limit his selection to two or three colours. It does not matter if the yarns are of different thicknesses.

Some weavers find it helpful at this stage to glue short lengths on to paper, laying the threads side by side to give the appearance of the stripe in the warp (Figs 24–5). This does not give an accurate number of threads per inch in the warp, but it does show the proportion of the warp stripe in the design.

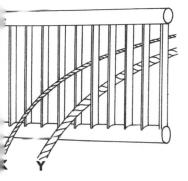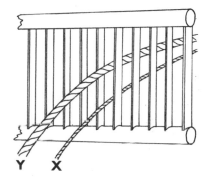

Fig. 28

Plain weave is the tightest weave, with the threads interlacing as much as it is possible for them to interlace, therefore the warp threads can be slightly more spaced out. Patterned weaving usually has less interlacing of threads forming the design, so the warp threads need to be set closer together to make a good construction and a hard-wearing fabric.

There are various tests which enable a weaver to judge very accurately how many warp threads he should have to an inch.

Choose a reed which appears to have a suitable number of dents per inch for the design. Thread the thickest thread through one dent of the reed, and slide it backwards and forwards to make sure it will move with ease through the dent. If not, a reed with fewer dents per inch will be required.

Place short lengths of the warp yarns side by side through the dents of the reed, arranging the threads in order of colour or texture to make the design of the warp stripe as desired. When using different thicknesses of yarn it will probably be necessary to vary the number of threads in a dent (Fig. 27). More than three threads in a dent may make the fabric look streaky, unless it is in an occasional dent in the reed for a particular effect in the design.

Check that there are not too many threads in a dent by making the threads pass one another in an up and down movement in the dent of the reed (threads X and Y in Fig. 28). If the yarn tends to stick, there are too many threads in a dent.

21

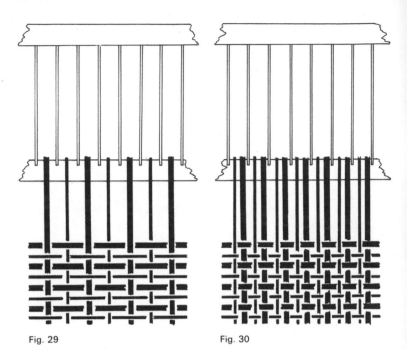

Fig. 29   Fig. 30

Try using one thick and one thin thread in a dent (Fig. 26) or two colours used alternately (Fig. 25). These are usually very effective in the design.

After placing short lengths of yarn in the reed, look at them closely. There should be a little more space taken up by the thread than there is space left between the threads (Fig. 30). (The only exception is oiled tweed yarn; these fibres will open out and take up more space after washing.) Tweed yarn should be set with the same amount of space used by the thread as space between the threads.

The importance of the sett of a warp is that well-constructed fabrics are either square, with an equal number of warp and weft threads per inch, or they have more warp than weft threads per inch, the weft often being a thicker thread than the warp. The only occasion for having more weft threads than warp per inch is when one of the wefts is used entirely for decoration and has nothing to do with the construction of the fabric. Once a weaver has learned to construct a good fabric, he can then add as much decoration to it as he likes.

Having decided the arrangement of the threads and the reed to be used, write down all the details necessary for making the warp, and check that the yarns are in the correct order to correspond with the design. The warp for a honeycomb weave is in the order of five thin threads followed by three thick threads, repeated throughout the warp (Fig. 24). For weaving a pattern also write down the draft for threading the loom, to make sure it corresponds with the arrangement of the threads in the warp. Fig. 31 is the draft for a honeycomb weave.

Decide how long the warp should be made, allowing at least half a yard's wastage for a table loom, and two feet for a foot-power loom, and some extra for shrinking, especially when using wool. For calculations see p. 102.

Honeycomb weave. Details for making the warp

Yarns: 2-ply Cambria welsh wool (2/16's wool) (Dryad Ltd)
 2/3's worsted
Finished fabric: 10″ wide × 2 yards long
Warp: width approximately $10\frac{1}{4}$″ wide
 length 2 yards + $\frac{1}{2}$ yard waste = $2\frac{1}{2}$ yards
Warp yarn order
Warp repeats: one repeat = 8 threads
 one repeat = 8 threads in 6 dents of the reed
 first repeat: 1 extra thread for selvedge
 last repeat: 1 extra thread for selvedge
Total warp: 17 repeats × 8 threads + 2 extra threads + 2 selvedge = 140 threads
Groups of threads for raddling: $\frac{140}{20} = 7$ threads per group ($\frac{1}{2}$ inch)
 $\frac{140}{20} - 3$ threads 1st group $\frac{1}{4}$ inch)
 = 4 threads 2nd group ($\frac{1}{4}$ inch)
Total warp: 20 groups of 7 threads (half inches)
Reed: 10 reed

Fig. 31

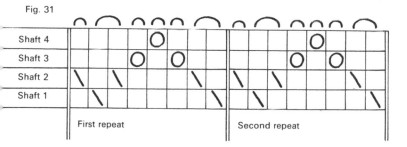

Making the warp

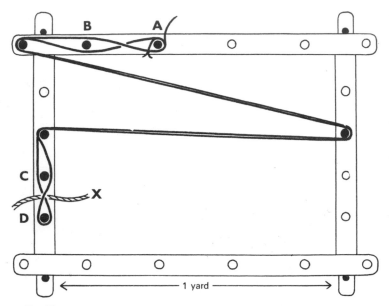

Fig. 32

Place the pegs in the warping board or warping mill (reel) the required number of yards apart. Tie the first thread loosely to peg A. Make the warp round the pegs with a cross (figure of eight) at each end between pegs A and B and C and D (Fig. 32). It is important to understand that the thread between peg A and D is one warp thread; Fig. 32 shows two warp threads.

A warping board is usually one yard wide. When measuring and placing pegs A, B, C and D extra pegs are required at one side or the other of the warping board for every yard added to the warp (Fig. 32).

When changing the colour of the warp thread, tie the two threads together with the knot as near to peg A or D as possible (Fig. 33). If alternate threads of different colours or texture are required in the design (this is often very effective), it is not necessary to break the thread off every time, the two threads may be run together in the warp and separated again for threading in the healds (heddles). When counting these threads in the warp do not

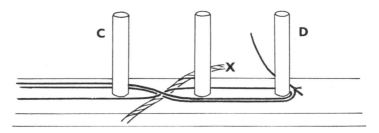

Fig. 33

Fig. 34

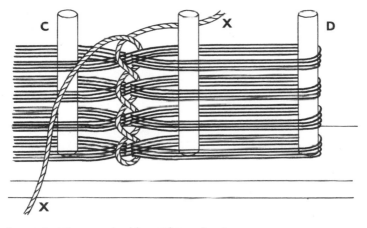

forget that they are double, and count as two.

The warp may have to be made in two halves if it is for a fabric 24" wide or wider. When making the second half, check that it is the same length as the first one.

Always count the warp threads in order of making them, where they cross between pegs C and D. For counting the threads into groups of half inches in preparation for raddling (Fig. 34), take a length of strong cotton (X), a little longer than twice the width of the warp, and place the cotton under the warp between pegs C and D (Fig. 33). After warping the correct number of threads for half an inch of warp, change the ends of cotton X across the warp, and again after the next half inch group, so that cotton X makes a continuous figure of eight round each quarter or half inch group at the cross (Fig. 34).

The honeycomb weave (Fig. 31) has twenty groups of seven threads, and one extra thread in the first and last groups for selvedge (Fig. 38).

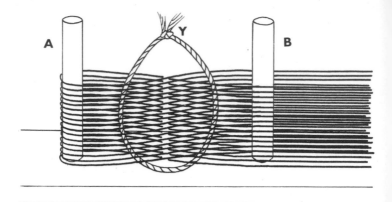

Fig. 35

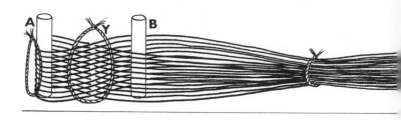

Fig. 37 Completed warp

Fig. 38 Cross section of the warp for honeycomb weave

When the warp is completed, it is most important to tie it correctly with strong cotton before removing it from the warping board or warping mill (reel) (Fig. 37). Tie a knot joining the ends of cotton (X) about one inch from the end of the cotton (Fig. 37).

Take eight inches of cotton, push one end down through the warp following the path of peg A, then up through the warp by peg B. Knot the two ends of cotton Y together (Fig. 35), this retains the cross in the warp. If the cross is lost, the order of the threads in the design has disappeared and the warp usually has

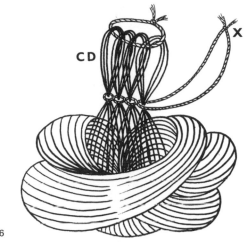

Fig. 36

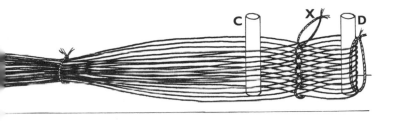

to be thrown away.

Tie the loop of the warp round by peg A and peg D, and then tie the warp tightly at intervals along the length (Fig. 37).

Check that the warp has been tied correctly, and remove from the warping board or warping mill (reel) by holding the end of the warp from pegs C and D, with the end pointing towards the elbow to prevent the warp from twisting. Wind the remainder round the fingers into a ball, tucking in the end from pegs A and B on the outside (Fig. 36).

Setting the warp on the loom

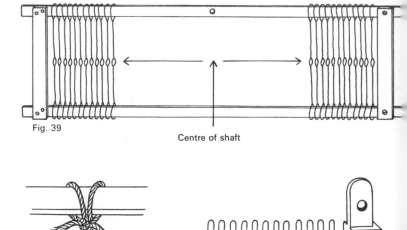

Fig. 39

Centre of shaft

Fig. 40   Fig. 41

Divide the healds (heddles) by pushing them back from the centre of the shafts (harnesses) (Fig. 39).

The front of the loom is recognisable by the sley or batten (beater) which holds the reed. Remove the top of the sley (beater) and the reed. Tie the raddle on the top of the back bar (beam) of the loom, so that it is unable to fall over (Fig. 41).

Place the warp on the table or a chair at the front of the loom. Take the end of the warp (C, D on Fig. 36), from the centre of the ball over the front bar, through the centre of the shafts (harnesses) and over the raddle on the back bar (beam) of the loom. Find the loop of the warp where it was tied at D and slide this on to the stick (apron-bar or stick) attached to the back (or warp) roller. Make sure the apron stick is tied to the back (warp) roller at each end and passes accurately through the loop of the warp. Cut the cotton tie at D (Fig. 37).

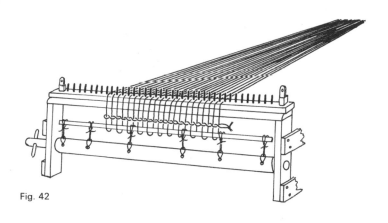

Fig. 42

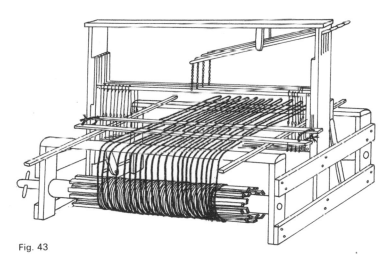

Fig. 43

Measure the raddle to make sure that the warp threads will be in the centre of the loom. For making samples a space will be left empty at each side. By holding the warp up under tension above the raddle with the left hand, it is now possible to see the half inch groups of warp separated by the cotton tie X. Start raddling on the right hand side by selecting the first group from cotton X and placing it between the pegs or nails of the raddle, then take the next group and so on until all the warp is through the raddle (Fig. 42). At this stage it is not always necessary but advisable to peg the top back on the raddle (Fig. 10 p. 13).

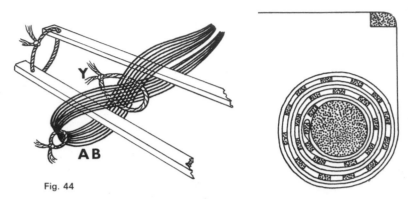

Fig. 44

Fig. 45 Cross section of the warp on the back roller (warp beam) of the loom

Spread out the loop at the end of the warp along the apron stick. Replace any ties which have been undone between the stick and the back (warp) roller, using the correct knot (Fig. 40).

From the front of the loom grip the warp where all the threads have been tied together, and give several firm tugs. Since the warp has been made on a loop this will even out the threads which may have been pulled during raddling.

On table looms with warps less than 24" wide it is possible for one person to wind on the warp by themselves, by holding the warp with one hand and winding with the other. With wider warps and foot-power (floor) looms, this can only be managed by hanging a weight on the warp near the floor, winding the weight up to the front bar of the loom, and moving it down again.

When two people are winding on a warp, the first holds the warp firmly under fairly hard tension. For warps 24" wide and over, the warp has been made in two halves and should be held with one half in each hand. As the warp is rolled on, the cotton ties are cut out, but do not on any account cut out the cross tie Y at the end of the warp, or the order of the threads will be lost. The second person winds the handle so that the warp goes once round the back (warp) roller; cotton X may be left in position to wind on to the roller. At this stage it is advisable to start winding in a layer of warp sticks or wrapping paper to give a smooth surface to each new layer of warp being wound around the roller. Wind the warp approximately three times round the roller and then place another layer of warp sticks, to prevent the edge of the warp falling down, and so on

30

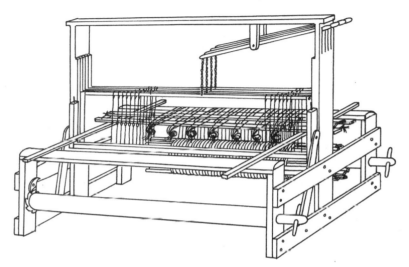

Fig. 46

(Figs 43, 45). When the cross tie Y is within three inches of the shafts, stop winding.

Remove the raddle. From the back of the loom carefully and accurately thread the cross or shed (lease) sticks through the warp, following the cotton tie Y (Fig. 44). Check that this is correct and remove cotton Y.

Rest the cross (lease) sticks between two long sticks placed each side of the loom from the back bar to the front bar (Fig. 43). Hold the loop at the end of the warp firmly and move the cross (lease) sticks back by pulling the threads below the front cross stick down. It is advisable to do this a section of warp at a time. When the threads are even and the cross sticks resting in the warp behind shaft (harness) four, cut out the cotton tie Y at the end of the warp (Fig. 44).

Cut across the loop of the warp in approximately one-inch sections, or cut right across the sections to remove any knots made when warping. Tie each section in a slip knot which is easy to undo (Figs 46, 50).

Threading

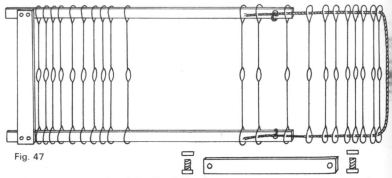

Fig. 47

Threading the healds (heddles)

When threading a loom it is important to sit in a comfortable position. On a foot-power (floor) loom remove the front bar (breast beam), so that a chair may be placed inside the framework of the loom.

Follow the threading draft and calculate the number of healds (heddles) required for the fabric (honeycomb weave, Fig. 53). Count the healds (heddles) from the centre of each shaft (harness), half on each side, and move the long sticks to the outside of the healds (heddles) to be used (Fig. 46). If there is room on the shafts (harnesses), spare healds (heddles) can be left empty at each end, though it may be necessary to tie these together with a piece of cotton to hold them out of the way. The empty healds (heddles) must not all be left at one end of the shaft (harness), as the weight tends to unbalance the shaft (harness), and this might interfere with the action of the loom when weaving.

Healds (heddles) may have to be moved from one shaft (harness) to another. Tie string healds (heddles) round the loop at each end before removing and placing on another shaft (harness) in one bundle (Fig. 51). Metal healds (heddles) can be changed in a group by removing the shaft (harness) from the loom and also the metal bar at the end of the shaft (harness) (Fig. 47). Tie each end of a length of fine, strong cotton through the holes at the ends of the shaft (harness) with a half hitch knot, then slide the healds (heddles) off the end of the shaft (harness) on to the cotton. The cotton is then tied in exactly the same way to another shaft (harness), and the healds (heddles) will slide on in their correct order (Fig. 47). This method is also used for storing metal healds (heddles) (Fig. 52).

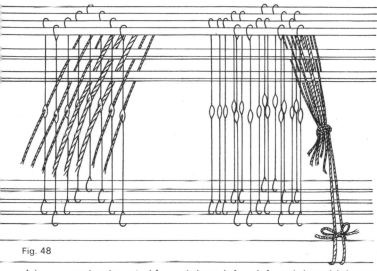

Fig. 48

A loom may be threaded from right to left or left to right, whichever is preferred. On some table looms the healds (heddles) can only be removed from one end of the shaft (harness). When this occurs it is advisable to start threading from the other end, in case healds (heddles) have to be added or removed during or after threading (Fig. 47).

When threading it is helpful to keep a section of warp under tension, by tying it with a loop of cotton to the front bar of the loom (Fig. 48). The same loop may be used for each section of warp.

Place the paper with the threading draft so that it is easily visible. Begin to thread the loom, by selecting the first thread from between the cross sticks and threading it with a reed hook through the eye of the heald (heddle) on the correct shaft. For honeycomb weave (Fig. 53), the first warp thread is drawn through the eye of the heald (heddle) on shaft (harness) two, the second on shaft (harness) one, the third on shaft (harness) two, the fourth on shaft (harness) three (thick thread), the fifth on shaft (harness) four (thick thread), the sixth on shaft (harness) three (thick thread), the seventh on shaft (harness) two and the eighth on shaft (harness) one. The design is then repeated continuously in the same order (Fig. 48).

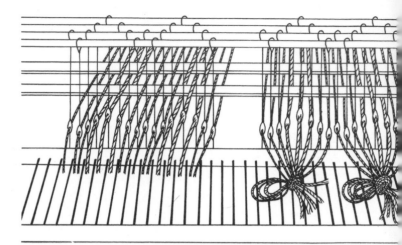

Fig. 49

The first and the last warp threads of the fabric should be threaded double through the heald (heddle) eyes, to make a firm selvedge.

The warp threads should not be pulled out from between the cross sticks, and should remain in the order of one thread over and one under each stick (Fig. 48).

After threading a group of threads, check that they are in the correct order, on the right shafts, and not crossed between the healds (heddles). Tie the groups in a slip knot (Fig. 50).

For threading a rigid heddle loom, the threads are selected in exactly the same way but threaded one through a hole and the next through a slot in the rigid heddle (Fig. 14 p. 14).

Sometimes it is quicker to thread string healds (heddles) with the fingers, especially when using thick yarns.

Threading the reed

Release the back (warp) roller and pull the warp forward through the healds (heddles) and the cross sticks about four to six inches.

Place the reed across the long sticks (Fig. 49), if possible at a level slightly below the level of the heald (heddle) eyes. The whole length of the reed may not be required for the fabric. Therefore measure the reed, to make sure an equal space will be left empty at each side. The weaving must be in the centre of the loom.

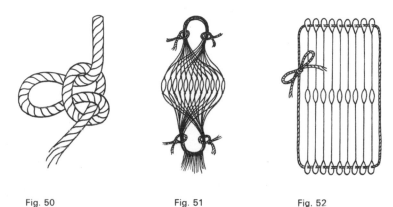

Fig. 50   Fig. 51   Fig. 52

Hold the first section of warp in the left hand above the reed, and the reed hook in the right hand below the reed. Select the threads in the same order as they were entered in the healds (heddles) with the fingers of the left hand, and pull the threads through the dents so that they lie side by side in the reed (Fig. 49). By following the original design of the warp it is possible to know whether there should be one, two, or three warp threads per dent in the reed (Figs 27, 31).

Release the back (warp) roller and pull the warp carefully through the reed, healds (heddles) and cross sticks until the reed will fit into the centre groove of the sley (beater). Replace the top of the sley (beater) to hold the reed in position. Remove the long sticks.

Fig. 53

				O				= 1 × 17 = 17 healds on shaft 4
			O		O			= 2 × 17 = 34 healds on shaft 3
\			\				\	= 3 × 18 = 54 healds on shaft 2
	\						\	= 2 × 18 = 36 healds on shaft 1

35

Preparing the loom for weaving

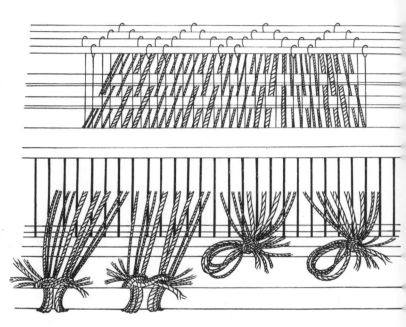

Fig. 54

Release the front (or cloth) roller until the canvas apron is covering the front cloth (breast) bar. Make sure the stick attached to this apron is securely tied with the correct knot (Fig. 40, p. 28). Release the back (warp) roller until the ends of the warp are long enough to tie round the stick.

Take a group of warp threads not more than one inch wide, and divide them in two halves. Place the two ends over the top of the stick and up on each side of the group, tie half a reef knot (Fig. 54). Continue across the width of the warp from the outside edge towards the centre, pulling the threads to make sure they have the same tension. Tighten each group by pulling the ends of the warp and tying a half bow. This time work from the centre of the warp to the outside edge. For good weaving the warp must have either an even tension or the outside edge slightly tighter than the centre.

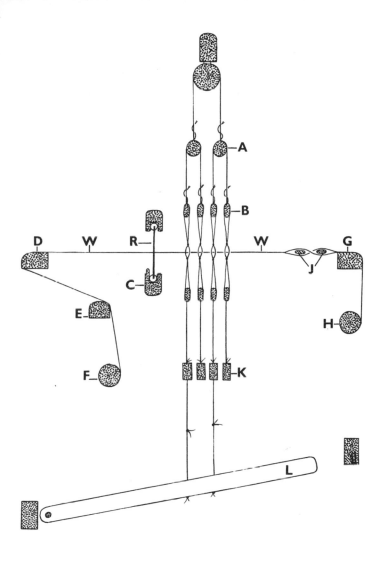

Fig. 55 Cross section of a foot-power (floor) loom. A—rollers, jacks or pulleys. B—shafts (harnesses). C—sley (beater). D—front bar (breast beam). E—knee bar. F—front roller (cloth beam). G—back bar (back beam). H—back roller (warp beam). J—cross (lease) sticks. K—countermarches or lamms. L—pedal (treadle). R—reed. W—warp

Fig. 56

Move the cross (lease) sticks back towards the back bar (beam) of the loom, otherwise they prevent the shafts (harnesses) from moving up and down freely for weaving. The cross (lease) sticks should remain in the warp during weaving.

Make sure all the shafts (harnesses) are on the same level and the warp is set in a straight line between the front and back bars (beams) of the loom (Fig. 55). If the warp is sagging down, raise the shafts (harnesses), by tightening the loom cord holding the shafts (harnesses) in position. Use one of the adjustable knots (Fig. 56 or 57). Check that loose ends of loom cord are not hanging down into the warp, or they may break some threads when weaving.

When preparing a foot-power (floor) loom for weaving, always start at the top of the loom and work down.

Make sure the top rollers or jacks of the loom are level (Fig. 55). Use adjustable knots in the loom cord.

Check that the shafts (harnesses) are level with each other, and fixed in that position. In Fig. 59 the shafts (harnesses) are held level at each end with a skewer through the holes at the end of the shafts (harnesses).

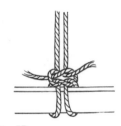

Fig. 57

Fig. 58

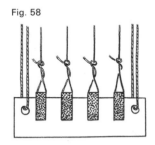

Fig. 59

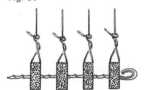

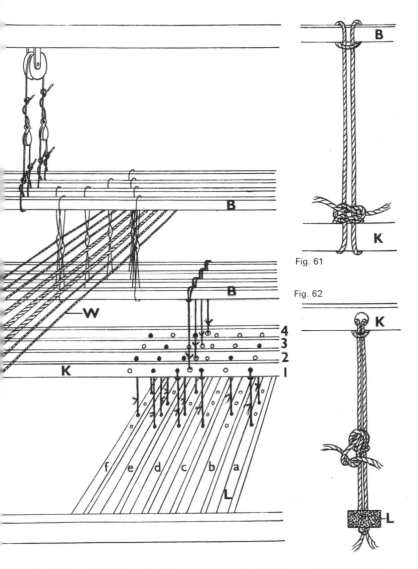

Fig. 61

Fig. 62

Fig. 60 B—shafts (harnesses). K—countermarch or lamm. L—pedals (treadles). W—warp

Fig. 58 shows the shafts (harnesses) held in position by shaft (harness) supports; these are also useful for holding the shafts (harnesses) level when threading the loom.

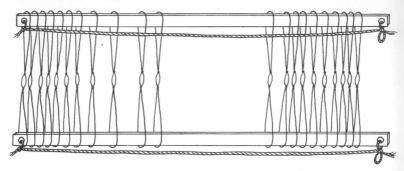

Fig. 63

Tie the centre of shaft (harness) number one to the first counter-march or lamm, making sure the countermarch (lamm) is at right angles to the side of the loom. Tie shaft (harness) number two to the second countermarch (lamm), keeping it level with the first, and so on, until the four shafts (harnesses) are tied to the four countermarches (lamms) (Figs 55, 60). Use loom cord with adjustable knots (Fig. 61).

Four-shaft (harness) foot-power (floor) looms have six pedals; when these pedals are pressed down, the countermarches (lamms) and the shafts (harnesses) they are attached to are also pulled down. When tying the pedals (treadles) to the countermarches (lamms) use the appropriate holes in the countermarches (lamms) and pedals (treadles) to make sure the loom cord is in a vertical position (Fig. 55). The pedals (treadles) should be tied to a height so that the end of the pedal (treadle) is approximately halfway between the level of the floor and the level of the countermarches (lamms) (Fig. 55). Tie the pedals (treadles) with thick loom cord, and use an adjustable knot (Fig. 62).

For pattern weaving refer to the draft of the design to see which countermarches (lamms) should be tied to each pedal (treadle) (Figs 60, 108, p. 63).

Pedal A is tied to countermarches 1 and 3.
Pedal B is tied to countermarch 2.
Pedal C is tied to countermarch 1.
Pedal D is tied to countermarches 1, 2 and 4.
Pedal E is tied to countermarches 1, 2 and 3.
Pedal F is tied to countermarches 2 and 4.

Pedals A and F, when used alternately, will give plain weave. Check that the string or metal healds (heddles) are unable to fall off the end of the shafts (harnesses). On wooden shafts holding string healds (heddles), tie a length of cotton across the shaft (harness) (Fig. 63).

Winding a bobbin

Cut some 3½" squares of medium thickness brown wrapping paper and round off the corners. Wind the paper tightly round the tapered spindle of the bobbin winder until approximately one inch of paper is left unwound (Fig. 64), then catch in the end of the yarn between the paper. Wind the handle of the bobbin winder with one hand, and hold the thread firmly between the finger and thumb of the other hand. Make a slight bump of yarn about ⅓" from each end of the paper (Fig. 65). Wind the yarn on to the bobbin backwards and forwards with a sideways movement of the hand; always keep a bump of yarn at each end of the bobbin, never taking the yarn over the highest point of the bump (Figs 66, 67).

Do not wind so much yarn that the bobbin will not fit into the shuttle. Pull the bobbin off the winder and thread on to the spindle of the shuttle with the end of the yarn through the slot at the side of the shuttle (Fig. 68).

If the yarn slips off the bobbin and gets tangled in the shuttle when weaving, the bobbin is wound too loosely, too tightly or at some point wound beyond the bump at each end of the bobbin.

Fig. 64

Fig. 65

Fig. 66

Fig. 67

Fig. 68

Weaving

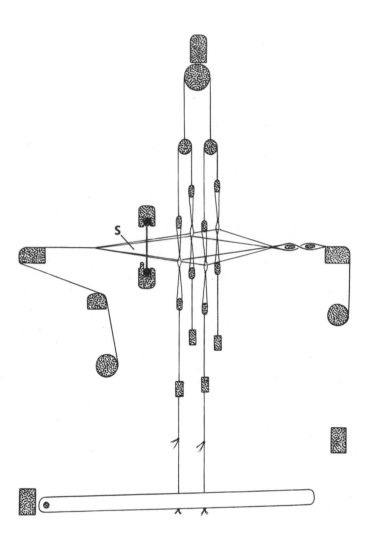

Fig. 69 Cross section of a foot-power (floor) loom. S—shed

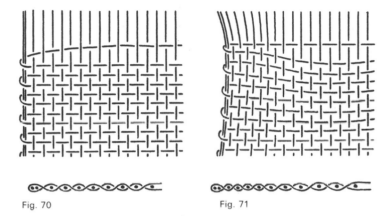

Fig. 70   Fig. 71

Loose threads are likely to break, so make sure the warp threads are reasonably tight. Move the cross (lease) sticks back towards the back bar (beam) of the loom.

Press down the pedal (treadle) of a foot-power (floor) loom, or the appropriate levers of a table loom; this lowers or raises some shafts (harnesses) and lifts certain threads of the warp. The space between the threads is known as the shed. The lower threads of the shed should be on a level with the base of the reed (Fig. 62). If this is not correct, the sley (beater) holding the reed will have to be raised or lowered or the shafts (harnesses) will need adjusting to the correct height (Fig. 55).

Pass the shuttle or stick shuttle through the shed of the warp as close to the reed as possible. This is the deepest part of the shed, so the weaver is less likely to catch the shuttle in the wrong threads and make weaving mistakes.

Pull the weft thread firmly to be sure the thread will not leave a loop at the edge of the fabric, while at the same time leaving the weft in a slight arc across the fabric (Fig. 70). The weft is going up and down, over and under the warp threads, as the cross section of fabric in Fig. 70 shows. If the weft is pulled across the warp too tightly, not allowing for this take up of yarn, the fabric will be pulled in from the edges. The warp threads at the edge become too close together, making the fabric tight at the sides, and giving the finished fabric a wavy edge. This makes the weft yarn curve, so that the cloth will not drape properly in a furnishing fabric and is very difficult to cut correctly in a dress fabric (Fig. 71).

43

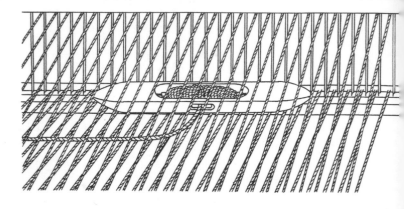

Fig. 72

After passing the weft thread through the warp, beat it back once into the fabric, by holding the sley (beater) in the centre to be sure the pressure is even. Change the order of the shafts (harnesses) according to the pattern, throw the shuttle across the warp, beat in the weft, change the shafts (harnesses) and continue weaving.

When a few inches of fabric have been woven, stop and count in the centre of the fabric the number of weft threads per inch. The warps of narrow fabrics and samples offer less resistance to the beat of the reed, so it is easy to beat in too much weft. There should be the same number of weft threads per inch as warp threads per inch, or preferably less weft than warp (Fig. 29 p. 22). Beginners will find they can weave quite evenly after completing about one foot of fabric.

When weaving with a roller (boat) shuttle, grip the shuttle between thumb and fingers with the palm of the hand facing upwards. With a flick of the wrist throw the shuttle through the shed of the warp, with the other hand in the same position at the opposite side of the warp ready to catch the shuttle. For pulling the weft firmly across the warp, the ring finger can be placed on the underside of the bobbin to put some tension on the thread. The slot of the shuttle should be facing towards the weaver with the rollers on the warp threads at the base of the warp (Fig. 72), if you have a shuttle with rollers. Otherwise the battons of the boat shuttle should be on the warp threads.

When joining the weft yarn when weaving, make sure the ends of the threads overlap (Figs 74, 75). Any loose ends may then be cut off.

When changing the colour of the weft yarn, it is possible to allow the different colours to loop up the sides of the fabric over short distances. If this is too untidy, end one colour and start another at the edge of the fabric (Fig. 73).

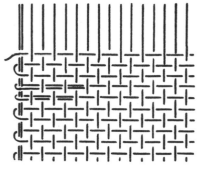

Fig. 73

For moving the warp forward, level the shafts (harnesses), slacken the warp at the back of the loom, wind the fabric forward on to the front (cloth) roller, and finally tighten the warp on the back roller. It is advisable to roll the warp forward little and often, since this prevents any marks showing across the fabric, and lessens the amount of wear and tear on the warp threads by the friction of the healds (heddles).

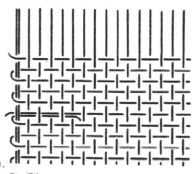

Fig. 74

Level the shafts (harnesses) and slacken the tension of the warp when the loom is not in use, to prevent the threads from being stretched continually.

Fig. 75

Always look at the fabric to see and feel the result of your weaving when the warp is no longer under tension. Examine the back of the fabric, sometimes it is better than the front!

Place a few loom sticks between the front roller and the fabric to cover any bumps where the warp has been tied to the roller.

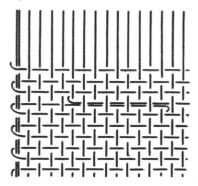

45

Fig. 76 Front of a four-shaft (harness) table loom showing sample of honeycomb weave

Fig. 77 Back of a four-shaft (harness) table loom set for weaving a sample of honeycomb weave and showing warp sticks between the warp on the back roller (warp beam)

How to solve weaving problems

Plain weaving in contrasting colours will show clearly any errors in the threading of the loom. A number of different types of mistakes may occur, some easy to correct, so examine the mistakes carefully before pulling out the warp unnecessarily.

When a warp thread will not weave correctly (Fig. 78) take the following course:

Look at the back of the fabric to see if there is a thread not being caught into the weaving. If so, follow its course through the dent of the reed and through the heald (heddle) to be sure that it has not been threaded through the wrong dent of the reed, in a different order from the healds (heddles). This will require changing the order of a few threads in the reed (Fig. 80).

The warp thread may not be through the eye of a heald (heddle), or it may be twisted round another thread between the healds (heddles) (Fig. 79).

If the thread is missing and the heald (heddle) is not missing, a section of warp will have to be rethreaded in healds (heddles) and reed. Occasionally a warp thread and the heald (heddle) is missing (Fig. 78). To make a heald (heddle), take a length of cotton, looping it round the lower bar of the

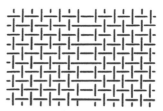

Fig. 78

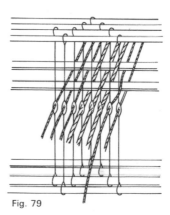

Fig. 79

Fig. 80

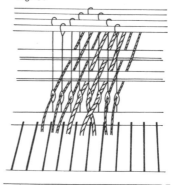

appropriate shaft (harness), tie a reef knot on a level with the base of the eye of the neighbouring heald (heddle), tie another reef knot on a level with the top of the eye of the neighbouring heald (heddle) and then tie the two ends of cotton over the top of the shaft (harness), cutting the ends off to about $\frac{1}{2}$" (Fig. 81).

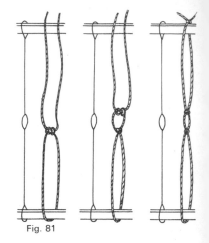

Fig. 81

Take a length of warp yarn, wind it round the back (warp) roller, thread it through the heald (heddle) that has been made. A space will have to be made for this thread in the reed, so a section of warp will have to be rethreaded in the reed.

When a thread has been threaded through a heald (heddle) on the wrong shaft (harness), this heald (heddle) will be left empty and a new heald (heddle) made on the correct shaft (harness) (Fig. 81).

If a dent has been left empty in the reed, a space will show along the length of the fabric (Fig. 82). This is usually worth correcting, by moving the threads along one dent in the reed. The same process should be carried out in reverse if there are too many threads in one dent (Fig. 83).

Sometimes threads stick together and prevent the warp from making a good

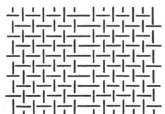

Fig. 82

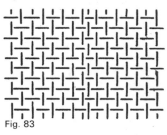

Fig. 83

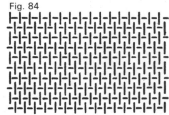

Fig. 84

shed. The warp may be too slack; or the sticking might cease after weaving the first foot of fabric, where the warp threads were handled when threading. If the warp continues to stick, the threads may have been set too close together in the reed (Fig. 84).

When there is a knot in the warp thread, it is usually impossible to weave over it. Treat as a broken warp thread.

To mend a broken warp thread, take the original warp thread to the back of the loom, leaving it in the cross (lease) sticks. Take a length of warp yarn, thread it through the reed and the heald (heddle), place it through the cross (lease) sticks beside the broken thread, and wind it about three times round the back (warp) roller. Place a pin in the fabric and wrap the warp thread round it in a figure of eight, making the tension the same as the other threads in the warp (Fig. 85). Weave until the original warp thread is long enough to be threaded back through the loom and pinned to the fabric. These loose ends may be sewn into the fabric after it has been removed from the loom and before it is washed.

When the edge warp thread of the fabric does not weave when weaving twill

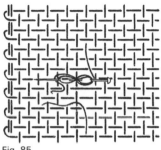

Fig. 85

Fig. 86

Fig. 87

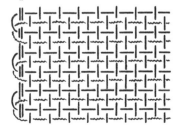

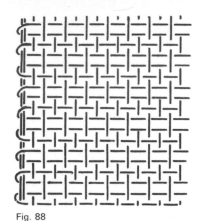

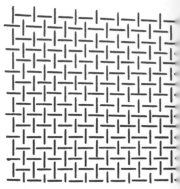

Fig. 88   Fig. 89

weave, try breaking off the weft and starting it again from the other side of the fabric (Fig. 86).

When weaving with alternate colours, the edge threads will usually remain unwoven unless the shuttles are used in the correct position to make the weft threads twist round each other (Fig. 87).

For weaving two weft threads in the same shed, and when weaving some patterns (rib weave), it may be necessary to catch the weft yarn round the edge warp thread deliberately (Fig. 88).

If the weaving is crooked (Fig. 89), the sley (beater) must have been pulled against the fabric with more pressure on one side than the other. Or it may have been set in the wrong position on one side of the loom or has worked loose. One half of the warp may have a different tension from the other; check that the roller stick has not jammed on the side of the loom or ratchet wheel when rolling the warp forward.

If the shed is uneven and the shafts (harnesses) are not level when weaving, fix the shafts (harnesses) in a level position and check the tie up of the loom, starting from the top of the loom and working down, making sure every part is tied in the centre with cords at the same tension, especially between the pedals (treadles) and the countermarches (lamms) on foot-power (floor) looms. New loom cord tends to stretch and sometimes the knots slip.

When the shafts (harnesses) do not move up and down with ease when weaving, check that the loom cord has not slipped off the pulleys at the top of the loom, and that the lower bar of the shaft (harness) has not moved to one side so that it catches on the side of the loom or in the string healds (heddles) of another shaft (harness).

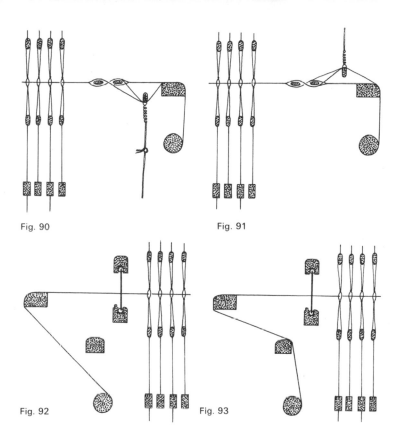

Fig. 90

Fig. 91

Fig. 92

Fig. 93

If a few warp threads or a section of warp becomes slack, place a rod over these threads and under the remainder of the warp at the back of the loom, behind the cross (lease) sticks. Tie the rod down at each end with an adjustable knot (Fig. 62 p. 39) to an expanding spring or piece of strong elastic to any part of the loom available (Fig. 90). The adjustable knot may be tightened at intervals when working, to continue to take up the slack of the warp. On some looms it is better to reverse the procedure and to pull the rod up and fix it to the top of the loom (Fig. 91).

When the warp is not over the knee bar of a foot-power (floor) loom, the weaver's knees will press into the fabric when weaving (Fig. 92). To avoid this, slacken the warp, remove the bar and replace it under the fabric (Fig. 93).

When the fabric does not handle well and feels like cardboard, there are usually too many weft threads per inch and possibly too few warp threads (Fig. 29 p. 22).

Plain weave

Plain weave, or tabby weave, is similar to darning. The warp and weft threads move up and down alternately throughout the fabric. This weave makes a firm construction of the fabric, since the threads are interlacing all the time (Fig. 30, p. 22).

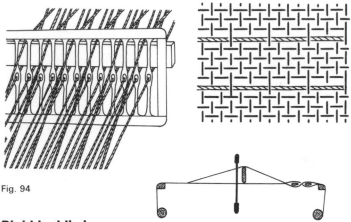

Fig. 94

Rigid heddle loom

This loom is limited to weaving plain weave only, with the warp set at 13 threads per inch, and is suitable for weaving woollen scarves and ties; also cotton table mats, belts, cushion covers and wall hangings, depending on the width of the loom.

With the warp always set at 13 threads per inch, a reasonable thickness of warp yarn has to be used, and cannot be varied to any extent. The weaver may vary the thickness of the weft yarn as much as he likes.

An interesting way to design on this loom is by changing the colour of the warp and weft, so making quite definite patterns with a combination of colour and plain weave (see pp. 82, 84, 87).

By using some imagination and ingenuity it is possible to break away from the limitation of plain weave on this loom. Try placing a stick about $\frac{1}{2}''$ wide behind the heddle under every other thread threaded through a slot of the metal heddle. Turn this stick against the metal heddle so that it lifts every fourth thread of the warp for weaving across a really thick weft yarn or a length of cane, etc. (Fig. 94). This technique may also be used for an inlaid effect, placing in an extra weft thread (thick) between every two plain weave weft threads (Fig. 95).

A lump of raw wool or a shaped piece of coloured acetate might be placed across the warp, but the shape should not be too wide, or the plain weave on each side of it will have difficulty in closing together.

When weaving, try selecting certain threads by hand; with some experimentation many variations can be obtained. You can obtain the appearance of a chain across the warp by looping a thick thread through sections of the warp selected by hand (Fig. 96).

A few tufts (knots) of yarn can be exactly the decoration required in the design. At least two warp threads are used for making the tufts (knots) on, and two weft threads are needed between each row of tufts (knots) to hold the tufts (knots) in position. If only a few tufts (knots) are placed in the fabric, two plain weave weft threads must be woven each side of the tufts (knots) to take up an equal amount of space to the tufts (knots) (Fig. 97).

Two-way (harness) loom

This is a loom also limited to producing plain weave, but all the techniques described for weaving on a rigid heddle loom may be applied to this loom. No stick can be placed

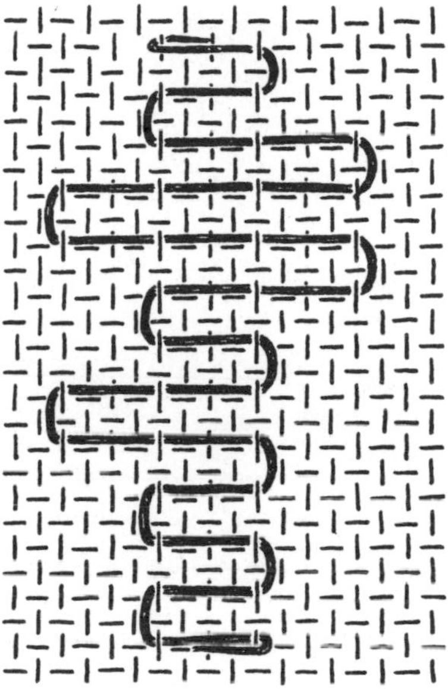

Fig. 95

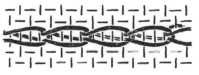

Fig. 96

Fig. 97

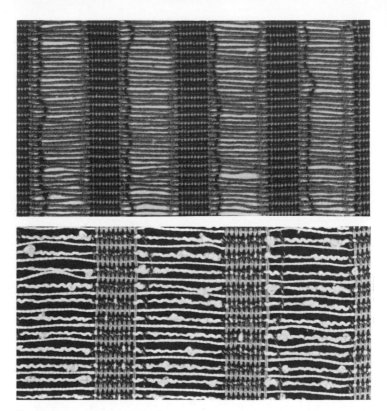

Fig. 98 Weave with threads slipping

Fig. 99 Weave with fancy yarn to prevent threads slipping, curtain fabric. Warp 3/18's (18/3's) light grey cotton, two threads used together as one, and 2/6's (6/2's) dark grey cotton, used alternately. Reed 16. 32 warp ends per inch in 10 dents, 20 dents left empty. Weft 2/6's (6/2's) white cotton and 1½'s white cotton gimp, used alternately

behind the shafts (harnesses) for raising every fourth warp thread, so one of the shafts (harnesses) must be raised and every other thread selected by hand.

The warp may be set with more warp threads per inch than a rigid heddle loom, so this gives more variety and scope for design. For instance, with the warp threads set closer together, the shaped piece of acetate or cardboard woven into the warp might be removed after the fabric has been woven, and this will leave a hole with only warp and one weft thread passing across it. This is very effective in a wall hanging, or for a cushion cover with a coloured lining.

A spaced warp with the warp threads set closer together than usual is interesting, especially for table mats with a cotton warp, or for wide scarves made with fine, soft wool. The warp must not be spaced when setting it on the loom, but should be spread evenly and spaced in the reed; this prevents the warp from piling up in bumps on the roller, and the weaver having to insert too many warp sticks.

Once the warp is set on the loom, there are many different ways of experimenting with it. Weaving plain weave with a smooth weft yarn tends to encourage the threads at the edge of each stripe to slip (Fig. 98). One way to prevent this is to use a fancy gimp yarn, probably in combination with a smooth yarn (to keep down the cost) so that the bumps in the gimp weft prevent the warp from slipping so easily (Fig. 99).

Another idea is to twist the warp by hand with a leno twist, and so create an interesting shape with holes between. A strong weft thread must be used at this point, because if the thread breaks the twist will come undone. On the loom the fabric appears to pull in at the sides, but after it has been taken off tension and

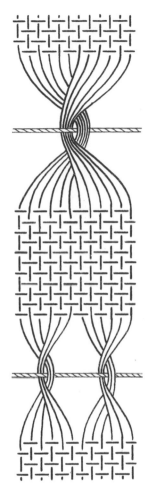

Fig. 100 Diagram of weave for Fig. 102

Fig. 101 Diagram of weave for Fig. 106

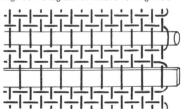

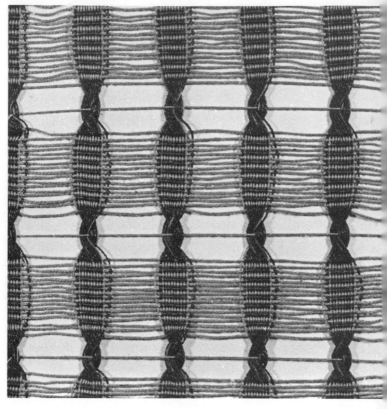

Fig. 102 Weave with a leno twist (diagram of weave Fig. 100), curtain fabric. Warp as Fig. 98. Reed as Fig. 98. Weft 2/4's (4/2's) grey cotton and 4/4's cotton (white)

pressed with an iron, it should be quite flat (Fig. 100).

For table mats, cane or raffia in the weft of a spaced warp is a good idea, and the mats can be washed.

Raffia mats are woven with a weft entirely of raffia, and the raffia which is sticking out beyond the warp at the sides of the fabric can be trimmed back to about $\frac{1}{4}$" of the warp after weaving (Fig. 103). One warp thread at the edge of the fabric will slip, and also one thread at the edge of each section of warp. These threads should be removed when the ends of the mat are knotted.

Cane mats can be made with round cane, flat band cane or a combination of both (Fig. 106). The cane must be damp when weaving, to keep it straight. Two plain weave cotton weft threads should be woven between each length of cane to make it secure. Pull the cotton weft tightly round the cane at the edge on

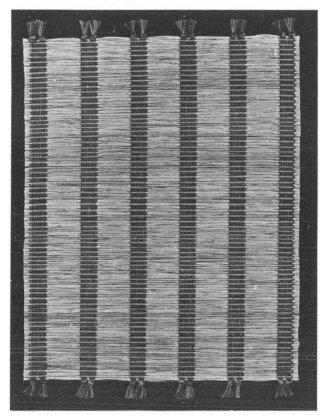

Fig. 103 Cotton and raffia table mat. Warp as Fig. 98. Reed as Fig. 98. Weft natural garden raffia

one side (Fig. 101).

When weaving table mats where the warp is knotted off at the ends, leave at least six inches of warp unwoven between the mats by weaving in some warp sticks and carefully removing them when about three inches of the next mat has been woven; this leaves three inches of cotton at the end of each mat for knotting.

The weft yarn on spaced warps must be beaten hard into the fabric, so the actual weaving technique is different. Pass the weft thread through the shed of the warp, beat it into position once with the reed, change the shafts (harnesses) and beat the weft back again before inserting the next weft thread through the warp.

Slacken the warp when looking at the fabric, as spaced warp weaving is deceiving when the warp is under tension.

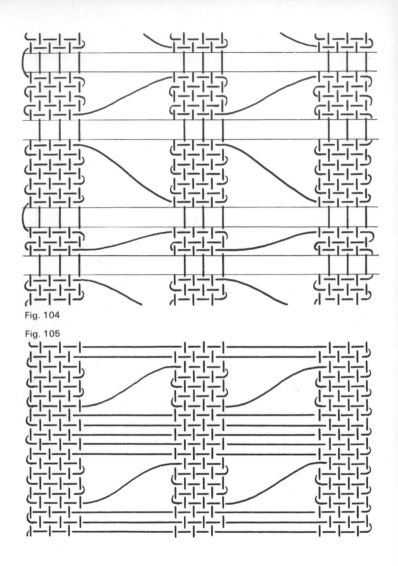

Fig. 104

Fig. 105

The weave shown on the title page is designed for a large wall hanging, and uses another technique suitable for a spaced warp (Fig. 104). This technique may also be used in combination with plain weave, and is suitable for curtains or a wall decoration (Fig. 105). This is slow work, as each section of warp is woven individually, by pushing the weft back with a hair comb.

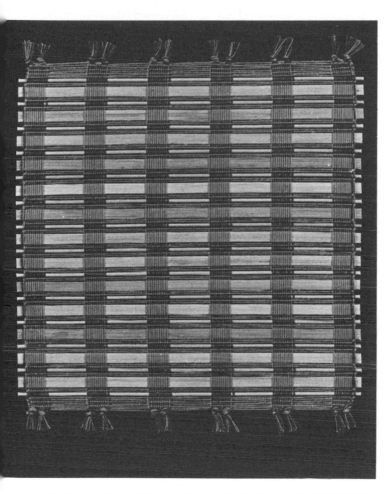

Fig. 106 Cotton and cane table mat. Warp as Fig. 98. Reed as Fig. 98. Weft 2/4's (4/2's) light grey cotton. Round cane and flat band cane

Four-shaft (harness) loom

All the techniques described for the rigid heddle and two-way (harness) loom can be achieved on a four-shaft (harness) table loom or a foot-power (floor) loom; the only difference is that instead of having to select warp threads by hand, the weaver can thread the loom so that the shafts (harnesses) will do the selecting.

Pattern-drafting

Pattern-drafting is not as complicated as it first appears to be. The weaver should persevere, and attempt to record all his work on graph paper. This not only enables him to keep a record of work, but gives him a much deeper understanding of the craft and eventually enables him to produce completely original design work.

The same honeycomb design has been used for instruction through this book and is shown in separate stages for drafting and analysis of the weave in Fig. 107. A careful study of this should enable the weaver to understand and develop designs from other books on weaving, where the drafting is sometimes presented in a different way.

A pattern is created by the order of the threads through the healds (heddles) on the shafts (harnesses) in combination with the arrangement of raising or lowering the shafts (harnesses).

Threading draft

Look at the threading draft (Fig. 108), which is the same as Fig. 31 p. 23. The spaces between the horizontal lines represent the four shafts (harnesses) when facing the loom from the front. The shaft (harness) nearest the weaver is called shaft (harness) one; in some pattern books this shaft (harness) is called shaft (harness) four, so the numbering is reversed. This makes no difference to the design, as the weaver can have the numbering whichever way he prefers. The mark in the square between the horizontal lines indicates the heald (heddle) on the shaft (harness) through which the thread should be placed. The 0 in the threading draft indicates thick threads. The horseshoe shape above the threads in the threading draft shows that these threads are placed together in one dent of the reed. (See mock leno weave in Fig. 124, p. 79 and honeycomb weave in Fig. 31 p. 23.)

Some pattern books give the threading draft as numbers, so the example in Fig. 108 would be shown as 21 2 3 4 3 2 1 . It is helpful to translate this into a threading draft on graph paper.

Treadling draft

The crosses in the squares between the horizontal lines indicate which shafts (harnesses) should be raised or lowered together or individually for weaving (Fig. 107).

Note that the shafts (harnesses) on foot-power (floor) looms are pulled down, and in table looms they are raised.

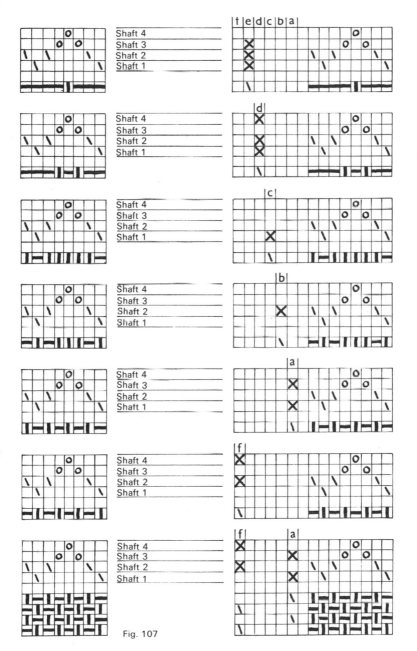

Shaft 4
Shaft 3
Shaft 2
Shaft 1

Shaft 4
Shaft 3
Shaft 2
Shaft 1

Shaft 4
Shaft 3
Shaft 2
Shaft 1

Shaft 4
Shaft 3
Shaft 2
Shaft 1

Shaft 4
Shaft 3
Shaft 2
Shaft 1

Shaft 4
Shaft 3
Shaft 2
Shaft 1

Shaft 4
Shaft 3
Shaft 2
Shaft 1

Fig. 107

61

For a foot-power (floor) loom, the crosses in the treadling draft indicate which shafts (harnesses) and countermarches (lamms) should be tied to the pedals (treadles) when facing the loom from the front.

Look at the treadling draft in Fig. 108. Shaft (harness) one is tied to countermarch (lamm) one, and shaft (harness) three tied to countermarch (lamm) three. Both these countermarches (lamms) are tied to pedal (treadle) A on the right-hand side of the loom. When this pedal (treadle) is depressed, shafts (harnesses) one and three will be pulled down. Refer to p. 36.

Many patterns have a plain weave weft between each patterned weft. It is helpful to have the left-hand side pedal (treadle) for one plain weave weft, and the right-hand side pedal (treadle) for the other plain weave weft. When the shuttle is passing through the warp from the left-hand side of the loom, the weaver knows that he must press the left pedal (treadle); and when the shuttle is going through from the right he will use the right-hand pedal (treadle). This simplifies the weaving and helps to prevent mistakes occurring (Fig. 107).

Order of treadling

This is the order in which the pedals (treadles) of a foot-power (floor) loom, or the levers of a table loom, should be used for each weft thread in the pattern (Fig. 108).

When the levers are pressed down, the shafts are raised when weaving on a table loom. Most books on weaving indicate weft on the face of the fabric, so the table loom weaver may wonder why the pattern has appeared on the back of the fabric! When using rising-shed looms and table looms read the blanks, not the crosses in the treadling draft (Fig. 108). It is usually easier to work the pattern from a column of figures showing which shafts (harnesses) to lift, until the pattern is memorised. 0 indicates a thick weft thread as in the warp. For example in Fig. 108.

	2	3	4
	1	3	4
	2	4	
0	3		
0	4		
0	3		
	2	4	
	1	3	4

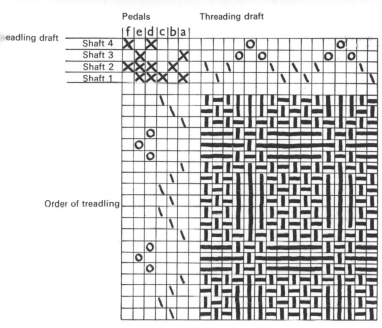

Pedals

Threading draft

Treadling draft

Shaft 4
Shaft 3
Shaft 2
Shaft 1

Order of treadling

Weave plan

Fig. 108

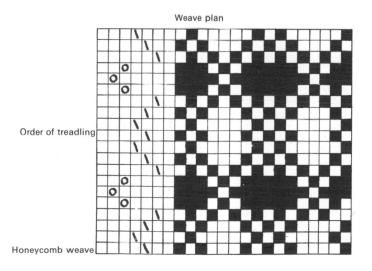

Weave plan

Order of treadling

Honeycomb weave

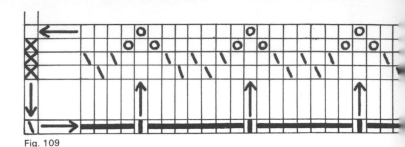

Fig. 109

Weave plan

This shows a detailed plan of the pattern, indicating which warp and weft threads are on the face of the fabric.

Weavers may find the method of vertical and horizontal lines for indicating warp and weft on the face of the fabric very helpful, especially when making up their own patterns.

Make sure that the warp threads in the weave plan correspond exactly with the warp threads in the threading draft, and the weft threads in the order of treadling from the treadling draft. Follow the arrows in Fig. 109. The first thread on shaft (harness) one is raised, so all the threads on shaft (harness) one are raised and indicated in the weave plan as warp on the face of the fabric, with the remainder of the threads on shafts (harnesses) two, three and four as weft on the face of the fabric.

When the weaver understands that when a shaft (harness) is raised all the threads on that shaft (harness) must be raised, he is then able to begin making his own designs, either by making a weave plan of a design and making up a threading draft to go with it, or by making other weave plans from an already established threading draft (Fig. 130).

When designs in books are given with no weave plan, it is a good idea to work one out on graph paper, so that the weaver can see the length of the weft or warp float of thread in the design and adjust the threading draft or order of treadling accordingly.

Photographs of woven designs are often deceiving, because the design is woven in colours that will photograph and gives no idea of scale in the design. The example in Fig. 130 has eight warp threads in the repeat, in six dents of a 10 reed, and therefore each repeat is $\frac{3}{5}$" wide. If this was woven in finer yarn in the warp, with eight threads in six dents of a 20 reed, the repeat would only be $\frac{3}{10}$" wide. The proportion of the design depends entirely on the thickness of the yarn and the number of warp threads per inch. The arrangement of colour can also change the appearance of the design entirely (see p. 82).

Pattern weaving

When pattern weaving on a four-shaft (harness) loom, so much variety can be achieved that it is often difficult for the weaver to know where to begin.

A beginner should start by threading his loom with a straight draft and then experimenting to see how many variations of weave he can achieve (Fig. 112). This will give him some understanding of how the loom works, and so enable him to progress to more complicated weaves and, later, to making up his own weaves.

Plain weave

The weaver should start by weaving some plain weave to show up any errors in the threading of the loom (Fig. 112A).

Twill weave

This is a well-known weave in woollen fabrics. A 2/2 twill has the weft floating over two warp threads and then under two warp threads (Fig. 112B). A 3/1 twill has the weft floating over three warp threads and under one warp thread (Fig. 112E). These weaves are of a looser construction than plain weave, so there is a danger of the weaver beating in too much weft; therefore the number of weft threads per inch should be checked.

Twill weave variations

These weaves are based on a twill weave, but instead of making continuous diagonal lines, the direction of the lines are changed (Fig. 112D). This idea may be used for breaking the twill weave into a more abstract design (Fig. 112J).

Satin weave

A useful weave for making the weft (Fig. 112F), or the warp (Fig. 112H), predominant on the surface of the fabric. Warp-faced satin and weft-faced satin can be used together to create a textured fabric with a horizontal stripe. This is interesting on a coloured striped warp, where the stripes of the warp predominate on the warp faced satin and the stripes are almost covered in the weft faced satin.

Where the weave changes, warp threads must interlock to prevent the weft slipping (Fig. 112L). The warp or weft-faced

Fig. 110 Herringbone weave, coat fabric. Warp 2-ply blue Wilton carpet wool, or other rug wool. Reed 12. 12 warp ends per inch. Weft 3/42's natural grey wool. 10 weft picks per inch

Fig. 111 Herringbone weave, coat fabric. Warp 2-ply Wilton carpet wool, or other rug wool, mauve, blue and dark purple. Reed 12. 12 warp ends per inch. Weft 2-ply dark purple Wilton carpet wool, or other rug wool

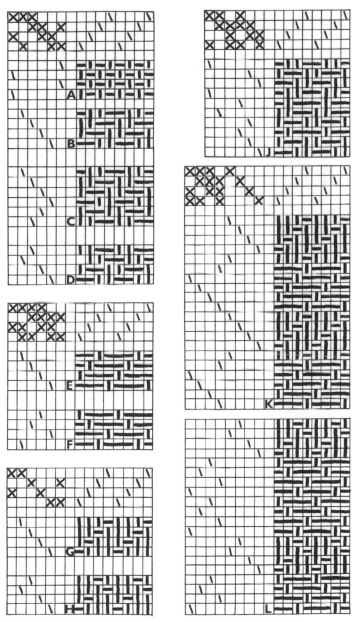

Fig. 112

satin weave may be repeated to make the required width of stripe across the fabric, but the weave must not be changed in the middle of the four weft threads which make the repeat of the weave, or the warp will not be interlocked (Fig. 112L).

A similar design can be produced by using a 3/1 twill weave and a 1/3 twill weave, to make this interlock the weave repeat is composed of five weft threads (Fig. 112K).

Herringbone weave

A herringbone weave is based on a twill weave, but the twill changes direction due to the rearrangement of the warp threads in the threading draft. This is an adaptable weave which can be used in many different types of fabric. The particularly interesting feature of this weave is that it can be changed to any proportion for designing, or even changed in proportion right across a wide width of fabric from one side to the other. This can produce fascinating ideas for dress, coat, or furnishing fabrics (Figs 111, 113).

Study Fig. 114 and note that the threading draft works on a system which is not too difficult to understand.

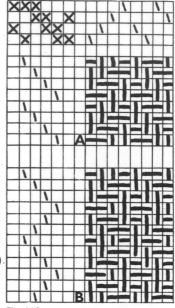

Fig. 113.

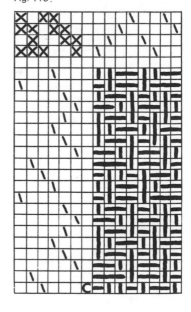

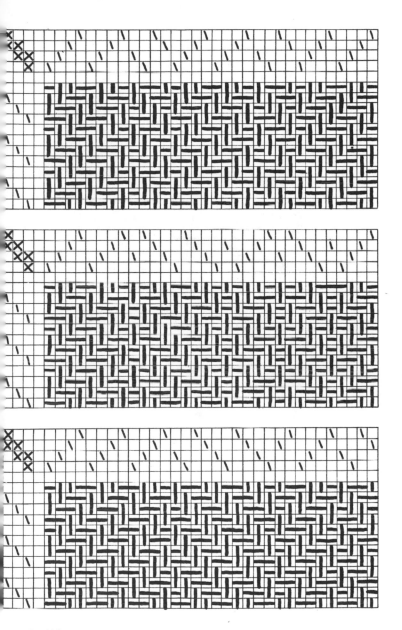

Fig. 114

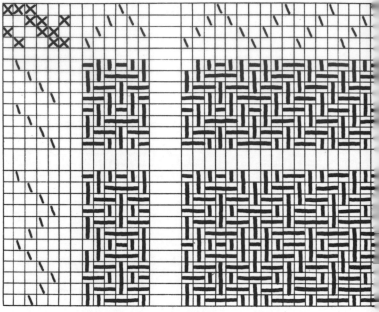

Fig. 115   Fig. 116

The pattern is strong when the warp is a different tone of colour from the weft, but two near tones make a very subtle effect. If a few threads of the same colour as the weft are placed in the warp, the weave tends to disappear, and this produces a strong vertical line of colour in the design (Fig. 111).

Try designing a coloured stripe in the warp which does not exactly fit the repeat of the change of direction in the weave, so that the weave is broken by the change of colour in the warp.

This weave may also be broken up in an abstract fashion, as described for a twill weave (Fig. 113C).

This threading draft is also used in combination with a 4/4 change of colour in the warp and the weft for a dogtooth (hounds' tooth) check pattern (Fig. 137, p. 90).

It is not possible to weave plain weave from this threading draft, since two threads come together on even shafts where the direction of the twill weave changes.

Diamond weave

This weave is based on a twill weave with the warp threaded to a point at shaft (harness) four and back to shaft (harness) one in the threading draft (Fig. 115).

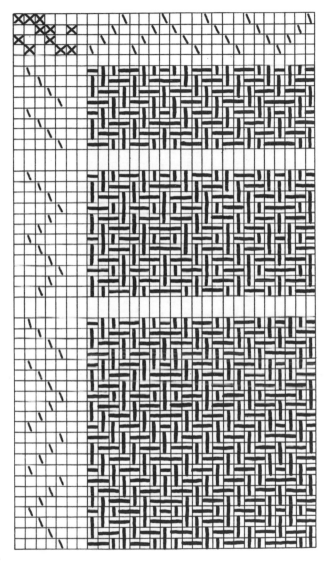

Fig. 117

The diamond or twill weave can be made irregular by adding some straight draft threading to one side of the point draft (Fig. 116). The diamond shape can be enlarged by adding some straight draft on each side of the point draft (Fig. 117).

Fig. 118 Draft for Fig. 119

Fig. 119 Dress fabric. Warp 2/7's blue mohair and 2/24's black botany wool, alternately. Reed 14. 28 warp ends per inch. Weft 2/7's blue mohair and 3-ply mauve wool, used alternately.

Figs 120 a, b, c Dress fabric made on same warp and using same weft as Fig. 119

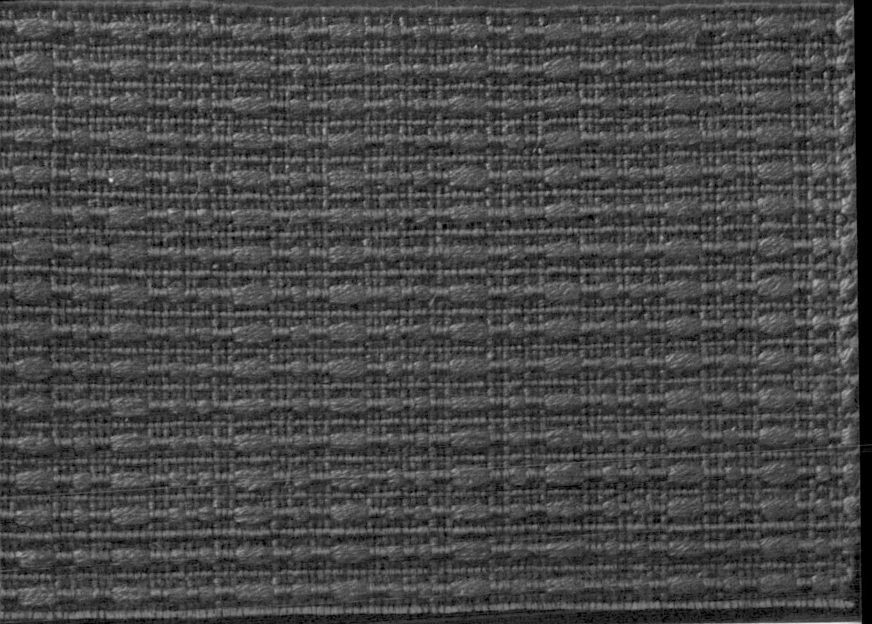

Fig. 120b

Fig. 120c

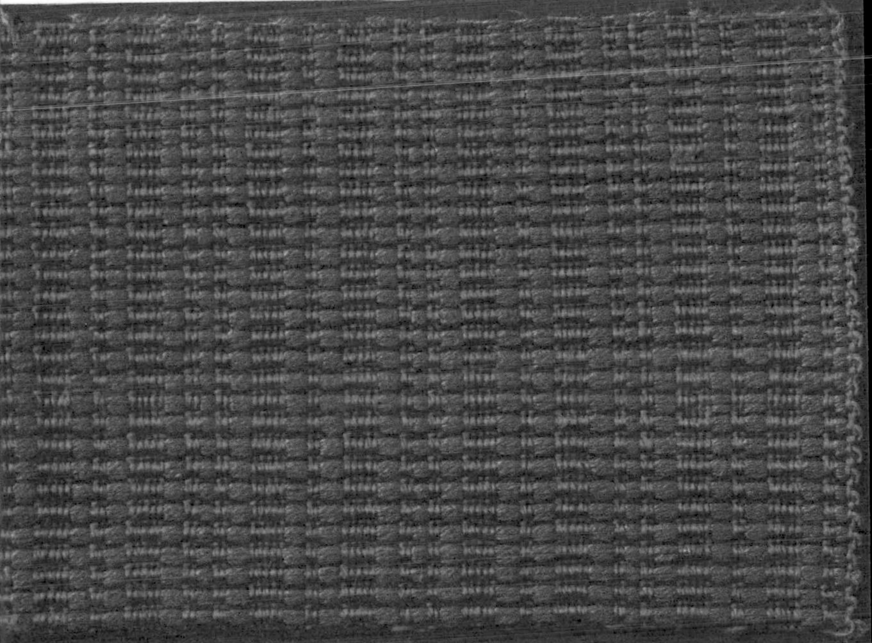

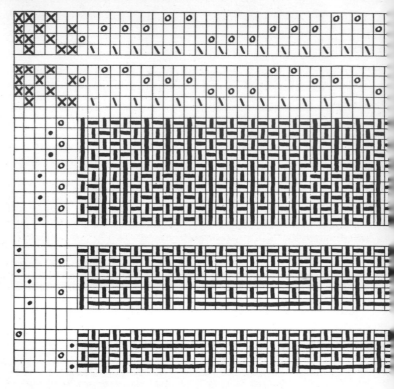

Fig. 121 Drafts for Figs 120 a, b, c. Threading draft as Fig. 118

This kind of arrangement of threads in the threading draft gives scope for experimenting with different weaves on the same warp; it is also a method which can be used for enlarging the design.

If the weaver studies these drafts closely, he will soon be making up his own designs. An interesting idea is to make a diamond pattern by figuring with the warp instead of the weft. This is achieved by placing a fine binder warp thread always on one of the four shafts (harnesses) between each thicker warp thread, which can be arranged in various ways on the remaining three shafts (harnesses). This makes a firm construction of the fabric, an exciting distortion of the weft threads and plenty of scope for making more designs on the same warp. The fabric designs in Fig. 120 are made on a warp of alternate threads of blue mohair and fine black botany wool; the weft is alternate threads of blue mohair and purple wool yarn. The thick and thin threads are indicated in the draft for these weaves in Figs 118, 121.

Rib weave

This is a useful weave for coat fabrics, and particularly good for upholstery and cushion covers.

Rib weaves are always woven with a weft binder thread, usually the same yarn and colour as the warp, and the pattern is made by a thicker extra weft thread. The binder weft thread is woven in plain weave, with one plain weave between every thick extra weft thread (colour plate on book cover and Fig. 122C). When designing this weave on graph paper, it is too confusing to show the plain weave between each thick weft thread; this is left out of the weave plan and only indicated in the order of treadling by the words, 'use plain weave' (Fig. 112C).

The interesting characteristic of this weave is that although it is possible to have two distinct colours in the design, the two colours do not mix by interlacing. This weave can often be tried on warps threaded for other weaves, with exciting results, and the ribs may vary in width in the repeat of the design (Fig. 123).

A distorted weft design may usually be woven on the same threading draft as a rib weave (Fig. 122D).

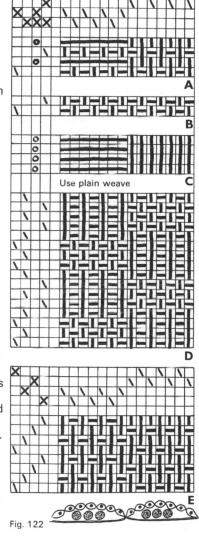

Use plain weave   C

Fig. 122

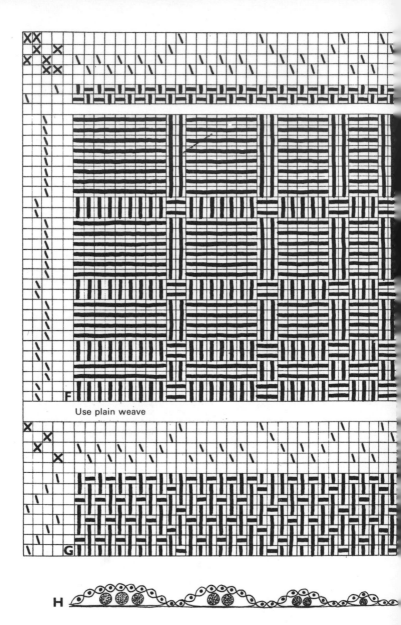

Use plain weave

H

Fig. 123

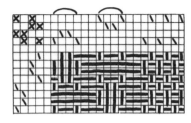

Fig. 124

Bedford cord

Bedford cord weave is closely related to a rib weave but the rib in the fabric is raised, making a ribbed texture instead of a change of colour. The weft must be an elastic type of yarn, so the warp can be made of wool or cotton and the weft of wool (Figs 122E and 123G). This design is most successful when woven in one colour.

The ribbed cord may be accentuated by stitching in a thick padding yarn, carpet or rug wool, between the weave on the face of the fabric and the floating weft threads on the back of the fabric, after the fabric has been removed from the loom (Fig. 123H).

Mock leno weave

Mock leno is an excellent weave for coat fabrics, blankets and pram rugs. Four threads of the warp are placed in one dent of the reed with at least two dents left empty between each group (Fig. 124)

A plain weave repp may be woven in a striped design in combination with mock leno (Fig. 124). Experiment on this warp by evenly spacing the warp through the reed and try some different weaves based on diamond and rib weaves (Fig. 125).

Fig. 125

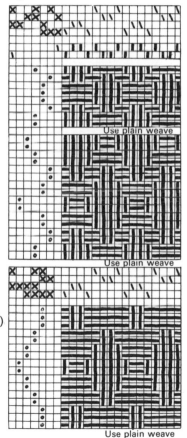

Use plain weave

Use plain weave

Use plain weave

Fig. 126 Coat fabric. Warp 2-ply white Cambria welsh wool (2/16's wool), Dryad Handicrafts, 15 warp ends per inch, and $2/2\frac{1}{2}$'s green worsted, 10 warp ends per inch. Reed 10. Weft 2-ply white Cambria welsh wool (2/16's wool) and $2/2\frac{1}{2}$'s green worsted. Honeycomb weave, as used throughout this book as example

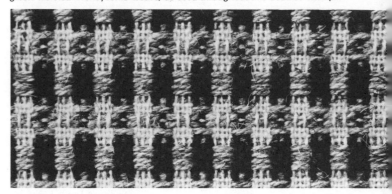

Fig. 127 Warp as Fig. 126. Weft 2-ply grey carpet wool and 2-ply white Cambria welsh wool

Fig. 128 Coat fabric. Warp as Fig. 126. Reed as Fig. 126. Weft 2-ply white Cambria welsh wool (2/16's wool)

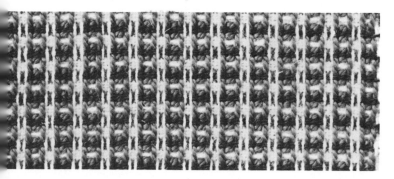

Fig. 129 Warp as Fig. 126. Reed as Fig. 126. Weft 2-ply white Cambria welsh wool (2/16's wool), 11 cut green Cheviot wool (wool tweed) and 2/2½'s green worsted

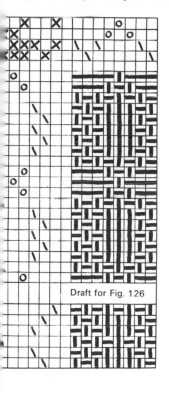

Draft for Fig. 126

Fig. 130 Draft for Fig. 128

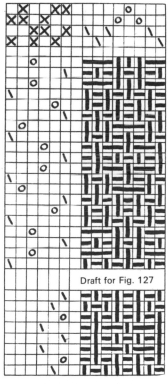

Draft for Fig. 127

Draft for Fig. 129

Colour and weave effects

Colour and weave effects describe themselves, since they are designs achieved entirely by the simple arrangement of two colours in combination with weave. A strong effect is obtained by using colours of a dark and light tone (Figs 133, 144), and a subtle effect by using colours nearer in tone (Fig. 139). A broken and interesting textured effect can be achieved by using some fancy gimp or slub wools in the warp and weft (Fig. 139).

These patterns are suitable for all types of woollen dress fabrics. The patterns can be worked out accurately on graph paper before the weaver decides how to set up a loom. Endless varieties of design may be made by using plain weave on a rigid heddle and a two-way (harness) loom, also twill and other weaves on a four-shaft (harness) loom. Several different patterns may also be incorporated in the design of one piece of fabric.

Designing these patterns on graph paper is really exciting. Apart from graph paper, the only equipment needed is a pencil, felt pen or coloured crayon, and possibly a pair of eyeglasses!

If necessary the weaver should refer back to p. 60 to make sure he fully understands how to read a pattern draft.

Write down the pattern draft with a weave plan (Figs 131, 132, 133). Indicate in the weave plan where the colour changes in the warp (X, Figs 131, 132). Indicate the colour change for the west in the weave plan (Y, Fig. 131, 132). To simplify the process, call these colours black and white.

Start reading across the first weft thread 1 in the weave plan (Fig. 131). Square 1A shows warp on the face of the fabric, and as warp thread A is a black thread, fill in the square with black. Square 1B is weft on the face of the fabric, and since weft thread 1 is black fill in the square with black. Square 1C is black warp, so fill the square in black. Square 1D is black weft, fill the square in black. Read across the second weft thread 2 in the weave plan. 2A = white weft, so leave the square white. 2B = white warp. 2C = white weft and 2D = white warp, and so on across weft threads 3 and 4. A complete range of designs using plain weave can be made in one fabric by changing the order of the colour in the warp and the weft (Fig. 133). This makes a useful sample for reference.

Try weaving two white weft threads before alternating them again (Fig. 131):
5A = black warp, 5B = white weft, 5C = black warp, 5D = white weft.
6A = black weft, 6B = white warp, 6C = black weft, 6D = white warp.

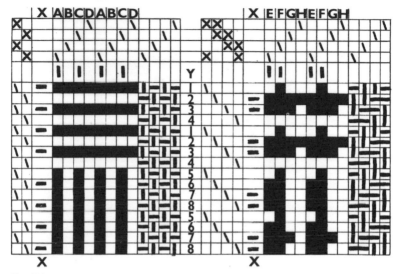

Fig. 131   Fig. 132

When weaving on a four-shaft (harness) loom, experiment on the same system with a twill weave (Fig. 132), with the warp made of two black and then two white threads (Fig. 132).

1 E = white weft, 1 F = black warp, 1 G = white warp, 1 H = white weft.
2 E = black warp, 2 F = black warp, 2 G = black weft, 2 H = black weft.
3 E = black warp, 3 F = black weft, 3 G = black weft, 3 H = white warp.
4 E = white weft, 4 F = white weft, 4 G = white warp, 4 H = white warp.

Fig. 132 shows the same idea with the colours of the weft starting in a different position in relation to the weave plan. This either reverses the direction of the pattern, or completely alters the design. Look at the design drafts sideways (Fig. 132) and notice that the same effects could be obtained the other way round by altering the position of the colour arrangement in the warp.

When working out colour and weave effects on graph paper, always leave a section of weave plan not filled in by the pattern, or make the weave plan show through the pattern, in case it becomes impossible to see the basic weave or to know where the colour is in relationship to the weave.

Fig. 137 is a colour and weave effect based on a herringbone weave, using gimp, slub and rough spun wool (Fig. 138) for white texture in the warp and weft. Where these yarns have been placed in the warp and weft is indicated in the draft for Fig. 139 in Fig. 137.

All these colour and weave effects are useful for giving a beginner an understanding of the combination of weave, design, colour and texture.

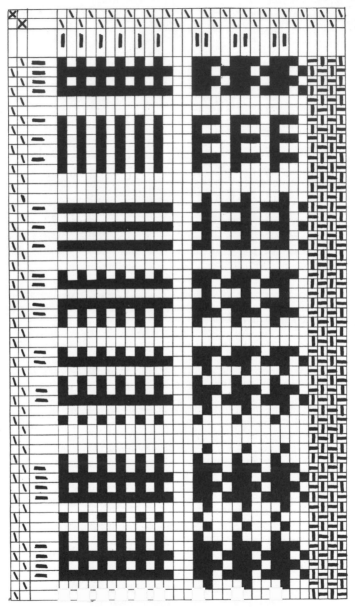

Fig. 133 Colour and *(opposite)* weave draft for Fig. 135.

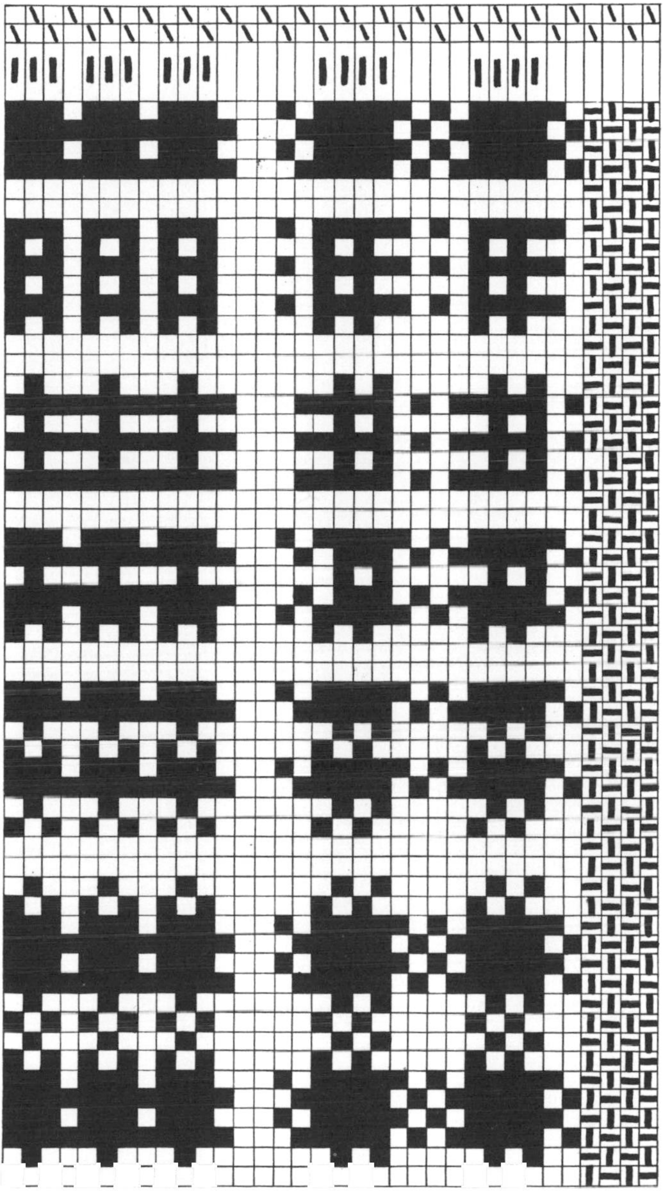

Fig. 134 Dress or suiting fabric. Warp 11 cut white cheviot tweed (wool tweed) and 11 cut black cheviot tweed. Reed 8. 16 warp ends per inch. Weft same as the warp. Details as Fig. 136.

Fig. 135 Dress or suiting fabric. Details as Fig. 133.

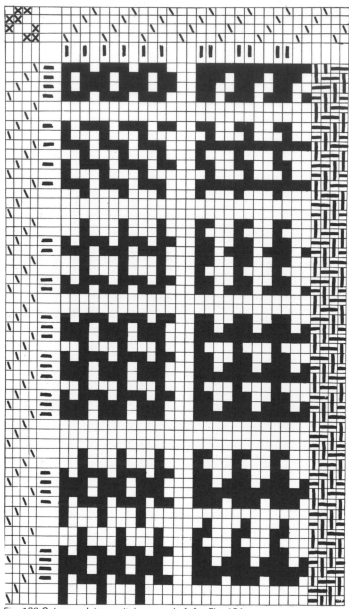

Fig. 136 Colour and *(opposite)* weave draft for Fig. 134

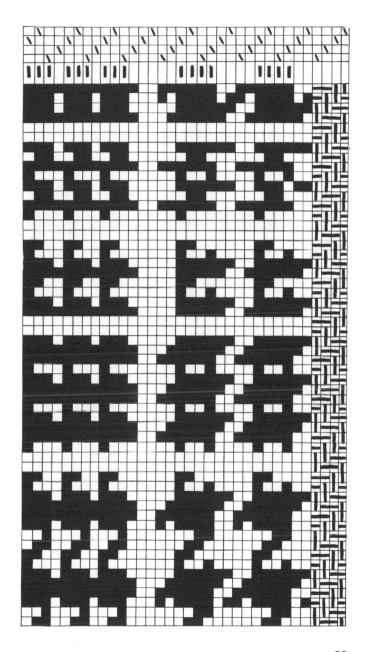

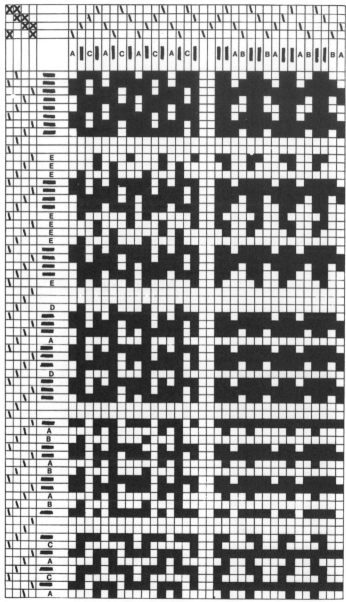

Fig. 137 Colour and *(opposite)* weave draft for Fig. 139

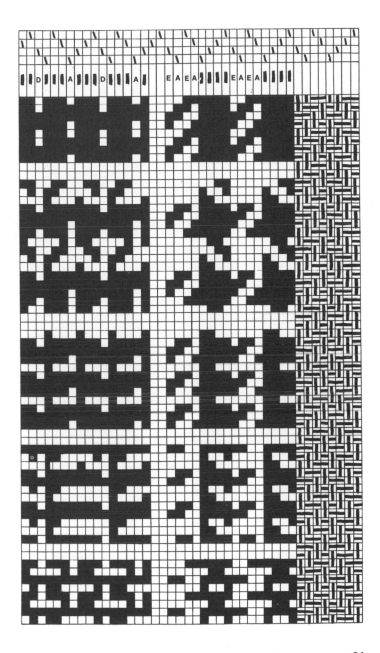

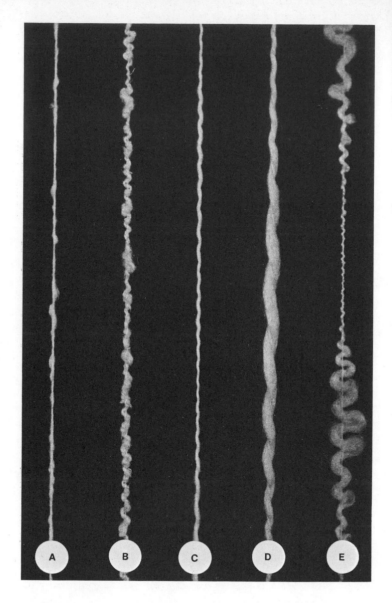

Fig. 138 Fancy yarns: A—white rough spun wool. B—white 2½ cut gimp wool.
C—white fine worsted slub. D—white worsted slub. E—white monstryl slub
boucle worsted

Fig. 139 Coat or suiting fabric. Warp 9 cut yellow welsh tweed (wool tweed) and 11 cut white cheviot tweed (wool tweed). White rough spun wool, white monstryl slub boucle, white 2½ cut gimp wool, worsted slub and fine worsted slub. Reed 10. Weft same as the warp.

Novelty weaves

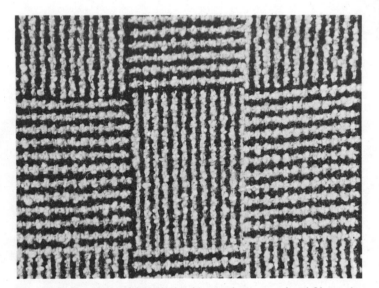

Fig. 140 Coat or blanket fabric. Warp white rough spun wool and 2½ cut gimp wool used together as one thread. 3/36's natural brown wool. Reed 6. 6 warp ends per inch. Weft same as the warp. 5 weft picks per inch

Fig. 141 Colour and weave effect draft for Fig. 140 using plain weave

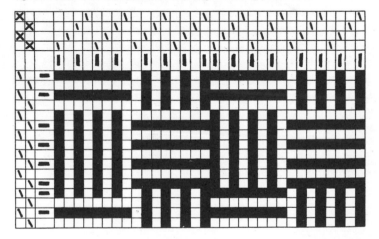

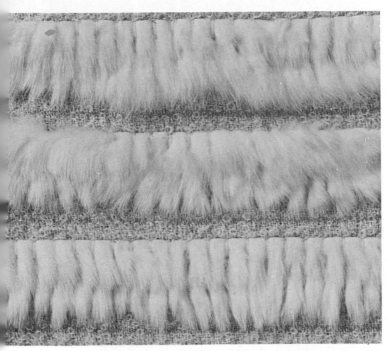

Fig. 142 Coat fabric. Warp 2-ply Cambria welsh wool (2/16's wool), white. Reed 8. 16 warp ends per inch. Weft 2's white looped mohair, silver viscose lurex boucle and ½" strips of cony rabbit fur cut across a plate of fur

Fig. 143 Draft for Fig. 142

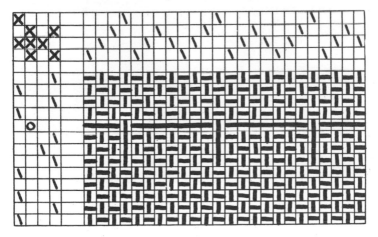

Fig. 144 Decorative dress fabric. Warp 2-ply white Cambria welsh wool (2/16's) dyed orange. Reed 8. 16 warp ends per inch. Weft 2-ply white Cambria welsh wool dyed orange and metalised P.V.C. (vinyl acetate) cut to shape (see Fig. 145)

Fig. 145 Cutting plan for Fig. 144

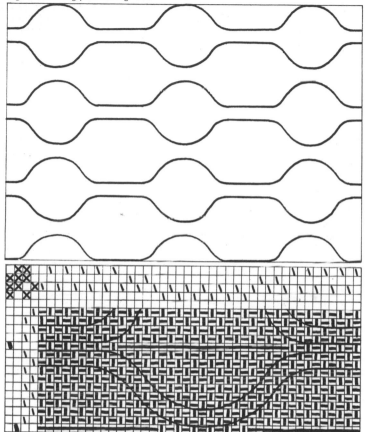

Fig. 146 Draft for Fig. 144

Metalised P.V.C. (vinyl acetate) or any other flexible material can usually be cut with several layers at a time. Fix the material to a sheet of thick cardboard with Sellotape, Scotch Tape or other adhesive tape. Place the cutting plan, drawn out on graph paper, on the top and cut through the layers with a sharp knife. Fig. 145. shows the cutting plan in half scale for Fig. 144.

The material used must be flexible enough to allow it to fold back against the reed when weaving, so that the weft will weave in under the shapes.

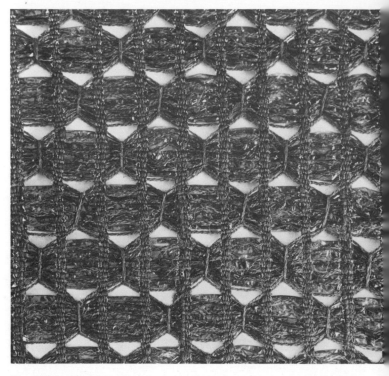

Fig. 147 Novelty fabric. Warp 3-ply blue wool and blue viscose lurex boucle, alternately. Reed 8. 16 warp ends per inch. Weft 3-ply blue wool and ½" wide blue cellophane

Fig. 148

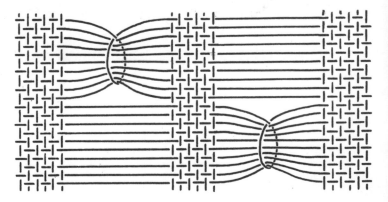

The finishing of woollen fabrics

Finishing is an essential process after weaving wool, before the fabric is made into a garment, and this applies particularly to fabrics woven with wool with oil and other impurities in it. The washing, apart from removing the oil, makes the yarn fibres open up, slightly matt together and causes a certain amount of shrinking. In a length of fabric approximately three inches per yard is shrunk in length and about three inches in width.

Woollen fabrics to be made into garments and woven with scoured wool usually improve in appearance with washing, and the shrinking that takes place will prevent the fabric from shrinking again after it has been made into a garment. All woollen garments should then be dry cleaned, not washed.

The only equipment necessary for the weaver to finish all his own woollen fabrics is a slatted roller about 12" in diameter, which he will have to make or have made. A solid roller is not satisfactory, because it does not allow the air to pass through it for drying the fabric (Fig. 151).

Once a roller has been acquired, finishing is a very easy process, but it is important not to matt the fabric too heavily. The weaver should know that there are certain things which will cause matting—too much soap, friction, or any sudden change in the temperature of the water.

Wash the fabric in soap flakes with plenty of hand-hot water, squeezing the fabric firmly all over. Do not rub or wring the fabric and do not use a detergent. Sometimes with oily fabric all the lather from the soap completely disappears. When this happens, remove the fabric from the washing water and wash it again in clean water with less soap flakes, to remove the remaining oil.

If a long length of fabric or a very heavy fabric has to be washed, try placing it in the bath and trampling it with the feet, this is good for the feet as well as the fabric!

Thoroughly rinse the fabric in water of the same hand-hot temperature. Spin dry or squeeze out surplus water.

Place the slatted roller across the bath or between two chairs, spread one end of the fabric across the roller, pushing the ends of the warp between the slats. Hold the fabric in position by tying a length of wood to the slat across the roller (Fig. 149). The wood of a new roller may mark the fabric, so it is advisable to fix a length of clean white paper round the roller first.

Turn the roller and start winding the fabric round it, at the same time pulling the fabric out at the sides and pulling it down in the front. Sometimes the fabric needs stroking firmly down round the

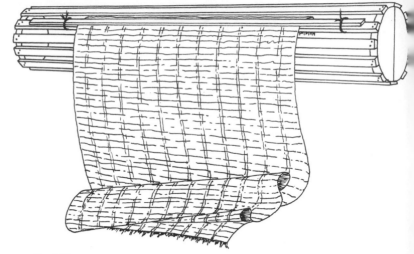

Fig. 149

Fig. 150

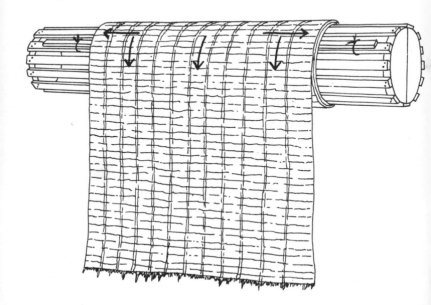

Fig. 151

Fig. 152

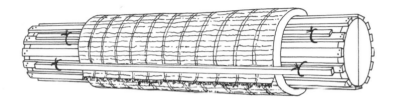

roller in the centre. Follow the direction of the arrows in Fig. 150.

The whole aim of this process is to set the weft at right angles to the warp, in preparation for cutting out the garment, so it is most important to have the edges of the fabric level and the weft in a straight line across the roller. This is not too difficult to see if the lines of the slats are followed. If the weft insists on curving, this may be due to having pulled in the edges of the fabric when weaving (Fig. 71 p. 43).

When all the fabric has been rolled onto the roller, secure the end by tying another stick to the slat of the roller and across the fabric (Fig. 152).

Allow the fabric to dry completely, quite naturally, in a room or the garden. Never place it in direct sunlight, or a change of colour may occur. An exceptionally long or heavy fabric may have to be removed from the roller and rolled on again with the outside end inside to allow the fabric to dry.

Most fabrics finished in this way do not need pressing. If the fabric does need pressing, always press it on several layers of blanket or something equally soft and place a piece of tissue paper on the top to prevent the wool from being polished. An interesting length or sample of weaving can be completely ruined by having the texture flattened out and then the surface polished by an iron.

Calculations

Count

The count is the term used to indicate the relationship between the length and weight of yarn.

The count number is the number of hanks contained in one pound of yarn.

For all ply yarns the count numbers are the count of the components.

Examples: 2/10's (10/2's) = two threads of 10's twisted together
= 5's

2/2's = two threads of 2's twisted together
= 1's

In spun silk the count number is for the ply yarn.

Examples: 2/10's = two threads of 20's twisted together
= 10's

2/2's = two threads of 4's twisted together
= 2's

Number of yards per hank (pound)

Yorkshire wool = 256 yards per hank (lb)
West of England wool = 320 yards per hank (lb)
Worsted = 560 yards per hank (lb)
Cotton = 840 yards per hank (lb)
Spun rayon = 840 yards per hank (lb)
Spun silk = 840 yards per hank (lb)
Linen = 300 yards per hank (lb)

Examples: 9 cut cheviot wool = 9 × 256 = 2,304 yards per pound
11 cut cheviot wool = 11 × 256 = 2,816 yards per pound
2/24's worsted = 12 × 560 = 6,720 yards per pound
4/4's cotton = 1 × 840 = 840 yards per pound
3/18's (18/3's) spun rayon = 6 × 840 = 5,040 yards per pound
2/20's (20/2's) spun silk = 20 × 840 = 16,800 yards per pound
2/8's (8/2's) linen = 4 × 300 = 1,200 yards per pound

Formula

epi = ends per inch (warp threads per inch)
ppi = picks per inch (weft threads per inch)

Warp: $\dfrac{\text{no. of epi} \times \text{no. of inches wide} \times \text{length in yards}}{\text{no. of hanks per pound} \times \text{no. of yards per hank}} = \text{pounds}$

Weft: $\dfrac{\text{no. of ppi} \times \text{length in inches} \times \text{width in yards}}{\text{no. of hanks per pound} \times \text{no. of yards per hank}} = \text{pounds}$

To remember this formula, think of the number of yards required for the warp or the weft divided by the count.

List of suppliers (England)

Ford Ayrton and Co. Ltd, Low Bentham, Nr Lancaster *(silk)*

J. Hyslop Bathgate and Co. Island Street, Galashiels, Scotland
(wool and cotton chenille)

Weavers Shop Ltd, Wilton Royal Carpet Factory,
Wilton, Nr Salisbury, Wiltshire *(carpet wool)*

The Hand Loom Weavers, Fourways, Rockford, Ringwood,
Hampshire *(cotton and botany wool)*

Cambrian Factory Ltd, Llanwrtyd Wells, Breconshire, Wales
(Welsh tweed)

T. M. Hunter Ltd, Sutherland Wool Mills, Brora, Scotland
(Scottish tweed)

Dryad Handicrafts, Northgates, Leicester
(wool and cotton and looms)

Hugh Griffiths, Brookdale, Beckington, Bath, Somerset
(wool and cotton)

A. K. Graupner, Corner House, Valley Road, Bradford 1 *(wool)*

Harriss Looms, North Grove Road, Hawkhurst, Kent
(looms and accessories)

List of suppliers (USA)

Shuttlecraft, P.O. Box 6041, Providence, Rhode Island *(silk)*

The Yarn Depot, 545 Sutter Street, San Francisco,
California 94102 *(chenille and other novelties)*

The Mannings, East Berlin, Pennsylvania 17316 *(rug wool)*

Troy Yarn and Textile Co., 603 Mineral Spring Avenue,
Pawtucket, Rhode Island 02860
(rug wool and assorted woollens and synthetics)

William Condon and Sons, 65 Queen Street, P.O. Box 129,
Charlottetown, P.E. Island, Canada
(wool—tweed effect and hand spun)

Contessa Yarns, Dept HW, P.O. Box 37, Lebanon,
Connecticut 06249 *(wool, cotton and synthetics)*

Charles Y. Butterworth, 2222 East Susquehanna Ave,
Philadelphia, Pennsylvania 19125 *(wool and cotton)*

Lily Mills Co., Dept. HWH, Shelby, North Carolina
(cotton and rayon)

Oregon Worsted Co., P.O. Box 02098, Portland, Oregon 97202
(wool)

School Products, 312 East 23rd Street, New York, N.Y. 10010
(looms and accessories)

Craftool, Inc, 1 Industrial Road, Wood-Ridge, N.J. 07075
(looms and accessories)

Index